Designing for Visual Aids

Designing for Visual Aids is a very practical
guide for designers and teachers. Andrew Wright
describes in detail the various visual media that play an
ever increasing part in modern visual education.
This book should do much to clarify the kind of brief
the designer has to extract from teachers - and so
enable him to present new, and often surprising, ways
of extending the teachers' aims.
In addition to establishing the part the design of
visual aids has to play in education today, the author
covers in detail the various media, such as overhead
projectors, slides and filmstrips, film, television
(including EVR), programmed learning and teaching
machines, wallcharts, wallposters and wallpictures,
magnetboard, flannelboard, hook and loop board,
and books.
This book should be of value to all graphic designers
and to everyone in the teaching profession.

Andrew Wright was trained in painting, lithography
and etching at the Slade School in London. He has
taught in France and England, and from 1963-69 was
Senior Artist on the Nuffield/Schools Council French
Project. He has written on the design of visual aids,
has lectured on the subject, and has written for
television.

Designing for Visual Aids

Andrew Wright

Studio Vista: London
Van Nostrand Reinhold Company:
New York

A Studio Vista / Van Nostrand Reinhold Art Paperback
Edited by John Lewis
© 1970 Andrew Wright

Published in London by Studio Vista Limited
Blue Star House, Highgate Hill, London N19
and in New York by Van Nostrand Reinhold Company
450 West 33 Street, New York, NY10001
Library of Congress Catalog Card Number: 79-109175
Set in 9/12 pt Univers
Printed and bound in the Netherlands
by Drukkerij Reclame N.V., Gouda
British SBN 289 79652 0 (paperback)
              289 79653 9 (hardback)

CONTENTS

INTRODUCTION

The extensive development since 1900 of the Visual Aids movement has been due to:
social and economic changes which have made new demands on education;
changes in educational thinking;
population increase leading to relative teacher shortage and need for greater efficiency;
a need to make the best use of the 'information explosion';
the possibilities presented by technological development.
These factors imply that the movement will continue to expand and also imply that more artists and designers will be needed in the future.

Who does the artist/designer work for?
educational publishers;
the state, eg. Services, Health, Safety in Mines, etc.;
curriculum development organizations paid for by eg. Nuffield Foundation, Ford Foundation, etc;
industrial training organizations;
university visual materials departments;
education divisions of private industry.

Which type of artist?
photographers and film makers;
TV graphics designers;
graphic designers;
illustrators;
designers in both two and three dimensions;
visualizers - ideas men.

Artists, as makers of materials for education, are teachers.
As such they must
a) have knowledge of what is going on in teaching;
b) be able to understand the particular teaching intentions they are involved with;
c) know of the technology available;
d) know their own craft and how it can best be used;
e) enjoy and appreciate the particular challenge of working for education.

PART 1

1. What is happening in Education?

OLD WAYS	NEW WAYS
Teacher centred	Learner centred
Class teaching	Group or individual learning; Child as active learner
Mainly determined by the adult's ideas on how a construction of a subject should be developed	Mainly determined by psychological basis of child development and learning
'Follow the text book!'	Consider the needs, readiness and interest of the child
External incentives (marks, stars, fear of punishment, etc.)	Internally motivated (curiosity, joy of discovery)
Imprisonment of rules	Exploration through free enquiry
A right way and a wrong way	Flexibility of method
'Get on on your own without talking!'	Discussion amongst children and between children and teachers
Largely private work	Deliberate attempts to communicate discoveries to others through graphs, models, talks, books
	Understand relationships and patterns
Learning by repetition	Use of wide variety of visual, kinaesthetic and other sense perceptions
Mainly verbal and symbolic	
Film show at end of term	Daily and purposeful use of audio-visual materials

The primary aim of contemporary education is to produce 'problem solvers'. Children being taught today will be adults between 1980 and 2030; the facts we can give them now may be 'old hat' by then. What we can do now is to help the development of the student's own ability to sort out facts, to develop curiosity, initiative, analytical and creative abilities.

Gone are the days when the teacher ladled from the tureen of knowledge into empty heads. Increasingly, opportunities are being created for individual development either through self-instruction (Programmed Learning) or by discovery methods and project work in small groups. In this type of group work the sense of self and of self related to the group can be developed.

When facts must be given as a basis for discussion or research, for example, then mass teaching may be the most efficient method.

Teachers' attitudes to school subjects are also changing. The 'interdisciplinary approach' and the 'integrated day' take the child's needs and interests as a starting point and acknowledge that this may often mean joining school subjects into more meaningful 'chunks' of life. In an environmental study, for example, Geography, History, Economics, Local Government Architecture might be involved.

An exciting and recent development is 'team teaching' in which a number of teachers group themselves and their children together into a working unit.

An example: 5 teachers and 200 children.

For pure information giving two teachers may take all 200 children for one period, leaving three teachers to prepare follow up material and situations. By alternating between large and small group teaching, most efficient use can be made of the teacher and, by working as a team, teachers may contribute at what they are personally best. Audio-visual materials for both mass instruction and for self instruction can make a valuable contribution with these teaching methods.

As a result of research into US rocket defence projects the 'Systems Approach' has been evolved. This concept has been adopted by industry and recently by education.

Although good teachers have always planned ahead, a total overall view of general aims as well as full attention to every aspect of a whole sphere of education (particular objectives, particular teaching techniques, and ways of learning) has rarely been tackled before.

The Systems Approach attempts this overall analysis, decides which are the most suitable methods, media and materials for any one part. This approach frequently leads to multimedia use. It is important, of course, that the individual teacher makes final adaptations to fit the material to his own group.

Massive projects, partly based on this concept, have been set up all over the world, they are called curriculum development projects, eg. Harvard Physics Project, the Nuffield Foundation Foreign Languages Teaching Materials Project.

The analysis of aims and means in the Systems Approach and in Programmed Learning development has given a powerful basis to all modern educational thinking. This 'task analysis' is essential for the production of all educational material and it is essential, therefore, for the artist to be 'in the know'!

Broadly, these are the questions we should have answers to before beginning work:

a. Who, as far as can be known, is the learner? Establish this in as much detail as possible (**The Learner**)

b. Where will the learner be when he receives the material - under a bwana tree in an Indian village square or crouched in a hooded, air conditioned, computer terminal booth? (**Learning Environment**)

c. Just what should the learner know or be able to do at the end of it all? (**Objectives**)

d. How should we as writers, designers and teachers try to bring this about? (**Teaching/Learning Sequence**)

1. Flash card used in language teaching.

2. The Learner

One of the first things to establish is the nature of the learner or group of learners. Individual psychological differences cannot usually be taken into consideration but some basic factors must be established:

age, type of intelligence, socio-cultural background and degree of readiness to tackle the problem.

Age

No one doubts that children perceive the world differently from adults. Yet it is usually not enough for the artist to be only generally aware of this. He must know in which ways his work, both method of presentation and choice of content might be affected.

What are the differences between the perception of children and adults?

Children of up to 12 years tend to take things quite literally, they tend not to conceive of abstractions but rather observe the concrete items of the situation.

Further, they often do not see any logical connections between various incidents, the ways in which one thing is related to another. This last characteristic applies to a situation represented in a single still picture and even more to connected incidents strung out through time which must be related together to produce an understanding of the whole, as in film.

It is probably only by the age of 12 that children begin to draw logical conclusions and make generalisations from presented data. Even adults who are not used to dealing with abstractions may be slow and inaccurate in their interpretation and conclusions.

A flash card (Fig. 1) depicting a boy at a desk reading from a book and at the same time writing produced the word 'work' from many adults who were able or wanted to generalise. Children of 8 tended to say: 'he is reading', 'he is writing', 'sitting', 'sitting with his legs crossed', 'he's got funny boots'.

The adults in this case were able to make a

10

2-3. Are they looking back the way they have come or looking through the next doorway?

collective summary of what the boy was doing. The children remarked on aspects of what he was doing.

In sequences of still pictures the likelihood that children will not connect the relevant incidents and make a logical account increases. In Fig. 2 taken from a sequence of 8, two boys are seen running across a room to a door. In the next picture (Fig. 3) they are looking round the door post. Are they looking back the way they have come or do we see them from the other side looking into a new room? In an experiment in a Leeds Junior School 60% of the 9 year old children were lost on this point.

In a film the situation can be worse still. Zazzo suggests that: 'It is only from 9 to 10 onwards that he can follow the order of the shots. Between a mental age of 10 and 12 he can follow the continuity in the sequences, but cannot grasp its significance. It is from a mental age of 12 that, in general, he can understand the film as a whole and becomes capable of grasping its central idea.' (as recounted by G. Mialaret)

Some perception problems which are put down to age may well be due rather to lack of the appropriate type of experience or, on the other hand, to a basically different type of intelligence. Vernon has shown that adults have difficulty in reading graphs. This may be changed, however, by the new approach to maths teaching in Primary School in which, increasingly, children are made familiar with the language and symbology of graphs and charts. In a few years time quite young children may be able to manage to interpret correctly graphs, charts, etc where untutored adults fail.

The subject or content of the picture or film as opposed to the style is often beyond the designer's control. However, it is worth remembering that there is no one more scornful than the child presented with something he has outgrown and equally not to be forgotten are the blank faces of children when content is pitched beyond their experience.

Respect for the subject in terms of authenticity and consistency is a necessity when working for children.

The most minor inconsistencies can undermine a child's whole confidence in the materials and the teacher will have to defend himself! In one sequence of pictures I was criticised by some 10–year old children for fractionally changing car door handles, wheel hubs, straps on sandals, and brief case locks.

Similarly, if a visual is to be in any sense informational then the designer must take into account children's almost obsessive interests in getting information out of visuals.

Schematic, sub-Impressionist, Expressionist or other personal 'handling' of style may prevent this happening. (*See Realism to Symbolism, Part 3*).

Intelligence

Some research has been carried out into the effect of intelligence (as measured by current IQ criteria) on interpretation of visual materials. Vernon has done a lot of research in the area of interpretation and understanding of graphs, charts and symbols. She concluded that the ability to interpret graphs depends not only on experience but partly on intelligence. Even the less abstract type of graph and chart, using photographs, pie charts, bar graphs may not be interpreted easily by average and less intel-

...igent people.

Leith in an experiment in 1967 compared the effectiveness of a ground plan of a Cyprus peasant farm with a 3-D realistic drawing of the same subject using grammar and secondary modern school children (See *Realism to Symbolism, Part 3*). He found that the less abstract illustration helped the secondary modern pupils' understanding and retention better than the abstract illustration.

The artist is unlikely to be able to influence the choice of content but he could advise on the type of representation and even on the whole approach.

Socio-Cultural Background

The way in which we are brought up will affect what we see and how we interpret it. Educational materials are often exported all over the world, it is therefore highly important for the artist to know where his work will be used.

Method of presentation

Some rather crudely printed drawings used for the teaching of English to Ghurka soldiers caused serious trouble when the sketchy shading lines on the faces were interpreted as caste marks.

There must be countless examples of misinterpretations of this sort, through the great variety of representational conventions which exist. However, it is particularly likely to happen when the stylistic convention is used fairly meaninglessly. Shading lines are a particular case in point. So often they are used as a vague gesture or used purely decoratively rather than to create form.

Keep asking, 'What is the familiarity of the learner in question with symbol conventions, cartoon conventions, film and TV conventions, layout and ways of reading a page, with typefaces', etc. Taking the last point as an example: Baskerville J italic is read as I on the continent of Europe.

Content

Different cultures may have radically different associations of meaning with objects and scenes. Misinterpretation or total lack of understanding may result.

The production of teaching kits for distribution in a great number of countries is therefore highly questionable unless they are easily adapted by the teachers.

There are also differences between near cultures which should be avoided. Asked to interpret a picture showing a French postman shaking hands with somebody while handing over a letter, an English girl suggested that the postman was congratulating him on having won the football pools. Daily hand shaking is unknown in England whereas in France it is a normal form of greeting.

Even within one culture there may be tremendous differences of response to visuals. It has been suggested that people who do not have to deal with abstractions in their daily jobs are more likely to gain from concreteness of theme, dramatic presentation and from personification.

Pupil Readiness

This involves not only his actual interest and willingness to pay attention and his type of thinking, but also how much he already knows of the subject. Just what can you count on? This the designer must establish and use as a reference point. It is often essential to keep returning to the aspect of the subject which is well known. Otherwise, the learner might become lost and the visual sequence quite irrelevant to him.

The cineloop sequence on Breathing (Figures 28-32) makes good use of this principle by going from the torso and the situation of the lungs to the detailed and rather abstract re-presentation of the 'buds' and returning along the same path.

3. The Learning Environment.
The Teacher's Role

The choice of medium will partly depend on the physical character of the learning environment and also on the equipment available.

African teachers find little comfort in the development of expensive technical devices, they may have to 'draw in the dust'. Figurines, wall charts and books (Part 2) may be as far as they can go.

The artist will also have to take into account how often the visual is to be used. Must it retain its visual interest or make only a momentary impact?

Is the visual to be seen near to or far away, in dull or bright surroundings?

The degree and type of teacher participation will affect the design of the material. If the teacher is present he can explain, he can direct attention and generally adapt the materials to the learner.

Self instructional material must be largely self-explanatory. In visual terms tremendous responsibility is put on the designer as a teacher to direct the student's attention, to make relationships clear, to establish degrees of importance etc.

14

4. Objectives

My objectives in this book are that the reader should know the characteristic features of contemporary movements in education; know the factors necessary to define a learning situation (eg. the learner, environment, objectives, methology intended); (Knowledge) be able to analyse the instructional intention of the people he is to work with; be able to identify, as far as possible, the various factors necessary for selecting and designing visual materials; (Analysis) be able to select visual materials and so design them and integrate them within the instructional sequence that they will make the optimum contribution from the point of view of visual materials; (Synthesis) be able to appreciate the quality and intentions of modern educational movements; (Appreciation) be interested in using whichever visual communicative skills he has in contemporary and future education. (Attitude)

The artist/designer must be given, or find out, as specifically as possible, what the objective is. What exactly should the student, apprentice, etc. finish up with at the end of the particular sequence in question? This knowledge will affect the artist's choice of medium and the design of it.

Types of Objective

As a result of the instructional sequence the learner will have acquired one or several of the following abilities or understandings, etc. The following are broad categories of educational objectives.

Knowledge:	1. Information, ie. facts and linked series of facts. 2. Principles and concepts, ie. understanding relationships of facts.
Analysis:	The ability to analyse a problem by identifying its components, the ability to relate principles that apply to it.
Synthesis:	The ability to solve problems and to produce new (to the learner) solutions and principles, and plan new products.
Skills:	Basically any action which has become automatic and no longer requires thought. These range from communication skills to craft skills.
Appreciation:	A new or developed appreciation and set of values about life situations, art, etc.
Attitude:	A new or developed active interest and personal opinion about life situations and problems.

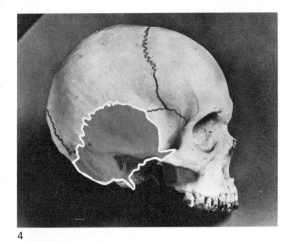

4

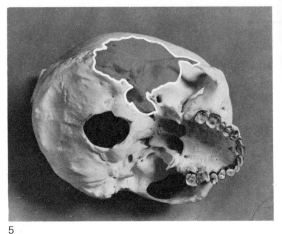

5

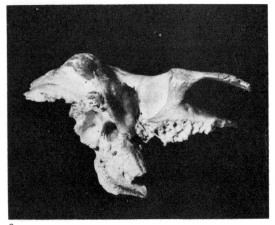

6

A Teaching/Learning sequence employing television and active student participation.

After an introductory presentation of the skull by the demonstrator the two photo stills Figs. 4 and 5 are shown highlighting the temporal bone from a familiar and a less familiar angle.

Fig. 6: both demonstrator and students have an example of the bone.

Fig. 7: the features and their relationships are isolated by this diagram.

Fig. 8: the student is given a labelled copy of the diagram for his future reference.

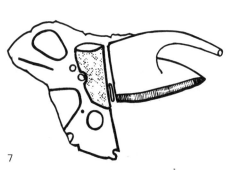

7

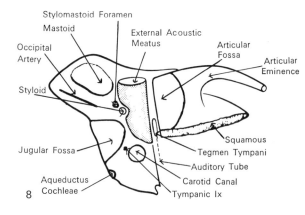

8

Stylomastoid Foramen
Mastoid
External Acoustic Meatus
Occipital Artery
Articular Fossa
Articular Eminence
Styloid
Squamous
Jugular Fossa
Tegmen Tympani
Auditory Tube
Aqueductus Cochleae
Carotid Canal
Tympanic Ix

16

5. Teaching/Learning Steps

What sort of processes can be evolved to help students successfully finish up with these objectives?

The procedure can be seen from either the learner's or the teacher's point of view, so, for convenience, I shall refer to them as Teaching/Learning Steps or Sequences.

The Teaching/Learning process will vary not only between categories of objectives, e.g. between knowledge and skills, but between different types of skills, different types of knowledge.

Other influences on the choice of the Teaching/Learning sequence will, of course, be the learner, what his attitude is, how much he knows already and the teacher's own preferences and intuitive judgments about 'what works best'. Whatever the sequence is, a primary consideration will be how people actually receive and absorb any piece of information.

Nobody claims to be able to define exactly how people do this, but the following may be a fair indication:

Firstly, the learner must be interested enough to pay attention.

Then he will be in a position to receive sense stimuli.

However, the brain will pick out stimuli according to preoccupation, personality, etc. These stimuli will be shuttled about and related to past experiences and ideas which have already been built up. The mind will try to find relationships between the new experience and the established ideas. These established ideas may be modified by the new experience. But if the new information does not seem to fit it will be thrown out.

If further aspects or examples of the new experience are received the groups of established ideas (concepts) may become further modified.

Then, if there is an opportunity for the person to use the newly formed concept, it will be more firmly grasped and more firmly retained. This is some sort of indication of how people learn. But what about teaching?

How would you teach someone how to take a photograph of silver cups, to design with type or to swim? How would you explain to older people about current pop music or to a foreigner about the peculiarities of our society? Would you start with lots of examples and then give him a summary of the basic idea, or discuss the principle first and give him the examples afterwards?

These two teaching strategies represent only two types of approach, there are endless variations of them. Much good teaching (and communication generally) is intuitive.

However, the conscious planning of a sequence of steps through which a learner will go will not cut out opportunities for intuition.

Too often the visual is chosen as being good for this or that objective without thought about how it will be used in one of these possibly lengthy and varied learning processes. Will the visual be just an example of something or will it summarise the idea?

However, there is more to it than just examples or summaries of principles.

The following chart might give a clearer example of the detail of teaching strategy which might be planned. Next to each 'step' is the type of visual which might be used at that point.

9. Objective   that the pupil be able to state the principle of expansion of solids caused by heat and be able to recognise the phenomena in real life and apply the formula.

Teaching / Learning Sequence:

General	Examples form real life.	
	Minimum commentary, maximum interest arousal	Film
Selective presentation	Teacher draws attention to the phenomena	Demonstration
Selective presentation	Pupils experiment	
General concept	General concept discussed by teacher and pupils	Overhead Proj.
Abstraction of concept	Stated by teacher	Overhead Proj.
		Chart or Book
Manipulation	Other examples of similar conditions, and exercises	Book
Discrimination	Other examples of rather different nature	Book (photos)
Summing up	Concept restated, with example, in a self-explanatory way	
	as memory jogger	Book

Because the idea of carefully planned sequences is most important for the designer and often not clearly stated or even known by the course writer or publisher, some more examples are given below.

10. Objective   same as above.

Teaching / Learning Sequence

Concept	Teacher states principle of expansion of solids	Blackboard
Selective Presentation	Some examples of the above in life	Slides
Selective Presentation	Pupils experiment	
General Concept	Teacher discusses whys and wherefores	
Abstraction of Concept	Teacher states formula	Blackboard
Manipulation	Exercises of examples	Book
Summing up	Formula stated	Book

Note: In none of these examples does a single step *teach* the objective. Each step, whatever it is based on, visual, discussion or experiment, will only make a contribution. *Thus the design of a visual will depend not only on the learner and the objective but on the particular contribution it is expected to make in the Teaching/Learning Sequence.*

11. Objective

that the pupil be able to understand and use the present tense of 'to sleep' in Spanish, in spoken and written form.

Teaching / Learning Sequence

General Presentation	New language introduced in a story sequence, giving it a real life context	Artist's Filmstrip and Sound tape
Selective Presentation	Teacher and pupils discuss what happened in the story sequence. The key section involving the new language is highlighted	Artist's Filmstrip and Sound tape
Selective Presentation	The pupils listen to the tape without visual support	
Discrimination	Pupils are questioned to establish their recognition of the new language	
Manipulation	Pupils act out the story sequence	
Discrimination	Written form within a new story context	Book
Manipulation	Written form. Various exercises	
Mnemonic	Statement of grammatical principle in written form to act as a reminder	Book

See illustrations on pages 20 and 21.

12. Objective

that the learner know of the methods of industrial soapmaking and of the chemical principles involved.

Teaching / Learning Sequence

General Presentation	The interest of the learner is first aroused by showing the variety of soaps and their significance in everyday life. He is also shown, in as realistic a way as possible, the industrial manufacturing processes	16 mm Film
Selective Presentation	The learner is now given the opportunity to study the ideas and processes by himself, at his own pace	Book
General Concept	Teacher and pupils discuss what the pupils have seen, heard and read	
Manipulation	The learner makes soap for himself by a method related to industrial process	Leaflet
Abstraction of Concept	The chemical process is stated in exact terms by the teacher	Blackboard, Overhead Proj. Book
Discrimination	With the pupils' new, though still shaky knowledge and experience the teacher and pupils look at the film again, in particular at the animated analysis of the concept	16mm Film
Mnemonic	Statement of the industrial process in a form useful for quick reference and as a reminder	Wallchart

See illustrations on pages 22-25

13.
Colour wash drawing of a sleeping Spaniard, used in film strip as part of a picture sequence for language teaching (see Fig. 11); used at the general presentation stage of the new language in a real life sequence.

14.
In the above black and white drawing, the distracting elements have been removed. It is used in the selective presentation stage.

15. The cartoon drawing is a memory aid.

16.
A still from a film on soap-making used at the general
presentation stage.

17

An eighteenth-century engraving used in a contemporary instruction book at the selective presentation stage.

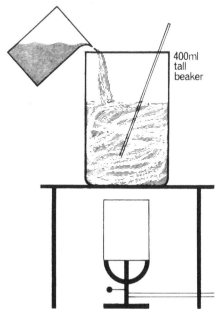

400ml
tall
beaker

Salting-out

18.
A diagram from a self-instructional leaflet on soap-making used at the manipulation stage.

Soap-making

Illustrated here is the batch production method of making soap. Although soap manufacture is now a continuous process, the basic chemical and physical operations remain the same.

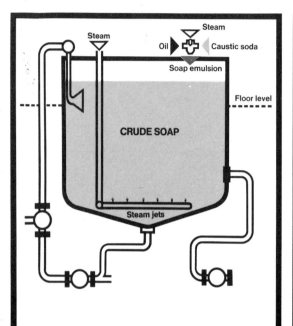

Steam

Steam

Oil ▷ ◁ Caustic soda

Soap emulsion

Floor level

CRUDE SOAP

Steam jets

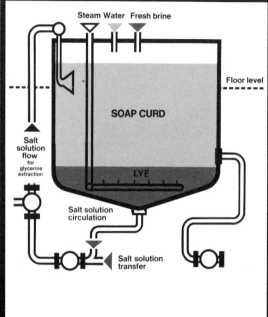

Steam Water Fresh brine

Floor level

SOAP CURD

Salt solution flow for glycerine extraction

LYE

Salt solution circulation

Salt solution transfer

1 Saponification

The heated oil and concentrated alkali solution enters the soap pan as an intimate mixture. The contents are boiled and steam is passed through to complete saponification.

2 Separation ("Salting out")

Salt solution is added to the molten soap and the mixture boiled up with open steam or mixed mechanically by circulation. When the contents settle, soap curd forms on top, with a layer of brine and glycerol, called lye, below. The lye is drawn off for glycerine recovery. Water and fresh brine are added to the mixture to remove more glycerine from the curd, and, after settling, the lye is again drawn off. This process is repeated several times.

19.
A wall chart to summarize and to recapitulate what has already been learnt.

A **UNILEVER** WALLCHART

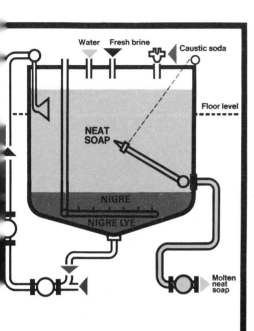

Water   Fresh brine   Caustic soda

Floor level

NEAT SOAP

NIGRE

NIGRE LYE

Molten neat soap

Fitting

ater, brine and caustic are added as required to bring
e mixture to the correct condition for the final stage. The
xture is allowed to settle for about 36 hours during
ich time it separates into:

molten neat soap which is drawn off through the
mmer pipe for processing into toilet soap, hard soap,
kes etc.;

nigre, a thin watery soap, which is left for inclusion in
e next batch;

nigre lye, which is drawn off through a tap at the bottom.

formation Division, Unilever Limited, 1959.   Revised 1966. Designed by Christine Brown, L S I A   Printed in England at The Curwen Press

Nuffield Foundation - Primary French.

Learner	
Age:	9-10
Intelligence:	average to above average (language ability)
Socio-cultural:	various within U.K. & U.S.
Subject readiness:	2cnd year of French (see Teachers Book for details)
Other readiness:	Familiar with use of visual materials in language learning.
Learning Environment:	Classroom
Max. viewing distance:	30'
Group:	35 pupils
Technical resources:	Few technical resources can be relied upon to be available.
Role of teacher:	Learning to be teacher lead.
General subject aim:	That pupils gain ability to understand and speak simple everyday French.
Particular Teaching / Learning objective:	That pupils be able to understand and use correctly 'toi', 'moi'.
Particular Teaching / Learning contribution expected:	the visual must combine with the audio tape to create the effect of a lifelike setting for the introduction of the new language, 'toi', 'moi'.
Visual aspect:	A number of visuals will be required in a sequence as the new language will be introduced in a short story. The visuals must be easy to handle by the teacher (repeatedly)
Economics. Cost:	The selling cost must ~~tool~~ be ~~great~~ kept to a minimum.
Production time:	10 days
cost:	—
Medium chosen:	A series of still images in the form of posters giving low cost and technical simplicity for the teacher.
Design:	Clear unambiguous shapes for easy recognition at 30'. Some degree of naturalism of depiction to give credability to the story.

PART 2

Part 2 is primarily intended as a glossary and introduction to visual media as used in education. In each of the sections will be:
a brief description of the physical characteristics of the medium and information indicating the type of technical apparatus which may be associated with it; following from these characteristics, notes on the likely use of the medium in the Teaching/Learning Sequence; observations on design and production with special relevance to work in education.

Note:
full technical instructions are not given, see further reading list,
those aspects of design shared by a number of media will be developed more fully in Part 3, e.g. readability, and viewing distance, use of shape, movement, etc.

OVERHEAD PROJECTOR TRANSPARENCIES

Description
One million overhead projectors are in use in the USA, approximately 100,000 in Great Britain.
The overhead projector is designed for use in daylight conditions.
The projected image size on the screen varies from 6 to 10 sq. ft.
Some overhead projectors can be adapted to show 35 mm film and 2 in. by 2 in. slides, e.g. Ofrex-Fordigraph.
In the UK the standard size of transparencies is 10 in. x 8 in., in the USA. there is considerable variation. Transparencies are either produced commercially or by the teacher using coloured markers, etc. Rolls may be used instead of sheets, but these are mainly for teacher production. Images made on transparencies vary from translucent lines, light resisting lines, colour transparencies or objects. The objects would appear in silhouette.
Technamation adds the possibility of linear and rotary movement at various speeds to a diagram using the application of polarized light with polaroid segments in the transparency and a rotating Polaroid disc before the projection lens.

Characteristics and Teaching Use
The overhead projector produces a static image. However, change can be shown and relationships built up by means of the overlaying of further transparencies.
Simple animation is possible.
Masks, overlays and animation help the teacher to control the learner's attention.
Technically, the overhead projector is easy to use. It can also be conveniently used with TV. It is essentially a device to enable the teacher to demonstrate an idea in simple terms and under his full control, unlike film which is a more 'self contained' type of medium.
In the Teaching/Learning Sequence the overhead projector is particularly useful for the limited presentation of an idea or process which can be reduced to a limited number of

21. The overhead-projector in use

LENS

PROJECTUAL

FAN

LAMP   LENS   MIRROR

22. Diagram of an overhead-projector

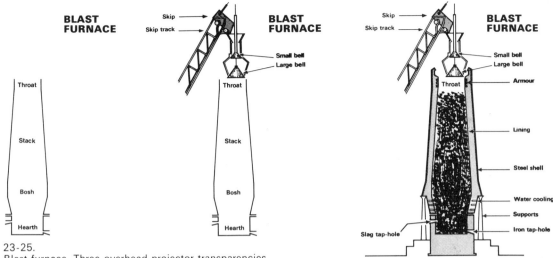

BLAST FURNACE — Throat, Stack, Bosh, Hearth

BLAST FURNACE — Skip, Skip track, Small bell, Large bell, Throat, Stack, Bosh, Hearth

BLAST FURNACE — Skip, Skip track, Small bell, Large bell, Armour, Throat, Lining, Steel shell, Water cooling, Supports, Iron tap-hole, Slag tap-hole

23-25.
Blast furnace. Three overhead projector transparencies, used as overlays to build up information.

stages and which must, at the same time, be seen in visual relationship with each other. The slide or filmstrip sequence, for example, cannot do this, the memory must hold the image of the previous frames.

Subject matters usually taken are the sciences and physical geography, however, there is no reason why the overhead projector should not be used in any subject area needing a simple analytical or synthetic approach.

Observations on Design and Production

There are a number of handbooks on the techniques of production for teachers.

Commercial transparencies are produced by lithography.

Outside mounts should be kept standard at 12 in. x 12 in. whatever the internal size.

Design specially for the overhead projector. Diagrams and serif typefaces designed for books are usually not suitable. The amount of information on a book page is also inappropriate for use with the overhead projector.

Keep the text to a minimum, this will direct the learner's concentration on the visual information. It will also permit the teacher to draw attention orally or to write on the transparency.

10 or 12pt Grot or Univers is recommended for use on s/s artwork. However, this will depend on the size of the projected image and the maximum viewing distance, (See *Legibility Part 3*).

Although the overhead projector is intended for use in daylight conditions the image is not always very good. Lines can easily disappear. It is advisable to make these fairly heavy, 1/16 in., and whenever possible to support them with a tonal or a colour area. Mechanical tints do not need to be coarse for this purpose - a common fault.

Tones should have a strong contrast.

Some colours are difficult to reproduce well, e.g. yellows and browns. Reds, blues and greens give good results.

Colour should be used for diagrammatic purposes, for motivation and to counteract eye fatigue. It should be remembered that background colours can hide the scratches·which will come with use.

Artwork should be clean and the transparency have no pin holes - cf. the large projected image.

Full colour transparencies are difficult and expensive to produce for the overhead projector. If possible, use slides. However, where a colour transparency is planned as part of an overlay sequence a high contrast film developed in ordinary developer will give the best results.

For negative images (white lettering) use contrasty films like Kodalith.

Masking and Simple Animation

The designer's own ingenuity will devise particular masking devices for each job. The idea is to control the amount of information projected, by flaps of card, by slides as for TV or pivoting discs.

For overlays in book form see Flipatran by Transart.

It is very important that whenever there is the slightest likelihood that the teacher may want to control attention by masking, the design of the layout on the transparency should allow for it.

SLIDES AND FILMSTRIPS

Description and Comment

The slide or filmstrip projector must increasingly be considered as the most common visual aid in schools, colleges and training centres. There are a number of other methods for projecting still pictures, for example, by micro-

projector or the opaque projector. The micro-projector enlarges and projects images from microfilm. A great amount of information can be stored on small pieces of film; it is possible to record the Bible on a piece of film the size of a postage stamp.

The opaque projector projects non-transparent material by the principle of reflection.

However, design considerations will not be so radically different for these media, hence no further mention will be made here.

Slides vary greatly in size, for example, American slides: 3 1/4 in. x 4 in., English: 3 1/4 in. square; Substandard slides 2 in. or 2 1/4 in. square.

Filmstrips are printed on 35mm film, the pictures on the strip vary from single frame 18mm x 24mm, 24mm x 24mm, to 36mm x 24mm double frame.

A recent survey of 70 secondary schools in Great Britain showed a tremendous variation between the sizes of projected images compared to the distances away of the farthest pupils. The average figure for this relationship, expressed in the number of image widths to the distance away was 8W (farthest pupil 8 widths away). Quite a number of schools used image sizes of only 2ft 6 in. width for children 30 ft away, i.e. 12W. These factors are most important in designing for easy readability. (See *Legibility, Part 3*)

Two new technological developments:

Photomotion, also called Diaporama, is an expensive device which directs two projectors to project images onto one screen. It has the technical potentials of dimming, linked mixing, wiping and twin iris controls. This device has been used effectively for T.V.

A far less expensive development than Photomotion is the slide or filmstrip projector linked to a tape recorder. An electronic pulse on the tape will move the next slide on. This combination of sound and picture gives the opportunity for pre-prepared teaching kits. It can be used as a self-teaching device for 500 students in a lecture theatre or for individual instruction. For self-instruction it is very convenient to use a rear projector (ie. the image is projected through the screen from behind). Projector, synchronizer, tape recorder and viewing screen may all be built into one unit (e.g. Frank-Kinderman machine).

Slides and Filmstrips compared:

Claims that one or the other of these media is the better per se miss the point. The choice between them should be made according to purpose.

Filmstrips are cheaper to produce per frame than slides.

Filmstrips are easier to handle than slides which invariably go in upside down. This is particularly important when the teacher is busy or inexperienced or when children might handle the machine.

Filmstrips control the order of frames. This again may be an advantage for inexperienced teachers or for self-instructional use.

Filmstrip frames cannot be replaced, if the information in one frame is out of date it may invalidate the strip as a whole.

Slides allow replacement of individual ones in a sequence through their being out of date, inappropriate or damaged. Also, the teacher can intersperse the commercially produced series with examples of his own.

Technically, slides can have better colour reproduction owing to possibilities of individual exposure. Strips are given a mean exposure setting. Slides, particularly if glassed, are less likely to be damaged.

Characteristics and Teaching Use

Filmstrips and slides offer the possibility of a large projected image.

Full colour is cheaper to reproduce than in other media, cf. books.

The image is still which may be an advantage. It is easy to mix photographs and artwork in a filmstrip or slide sequence.

The light image attracts attention. The relative darkness of the room hides shyness and frees emotions.

Film strips or slide sequences are very useful when presenting a subject for the first time or when developing the basic concept. The following example shows the possible variety of visual types, from photograph to diagram, within one slide sequence. The sequence is used to teach methods of analysis in medical training:

photo of patient in colour,

x-rays, electrocardiograms,

tolerance curves,

tables and lists,

diagrams.

Almost any of the objectives could be well served by filmstrips or slides, for example: facts in geography, science, biology; appreciation and attitudes: e.g. History of Art, Sociology.

These two media are not often used for the teaching of skills, though Laner's research (See p. 71) suggests that they would be often more suitable than film.

A sequence of stills lends itself to the representation of steps in a process, but only where the whole does not need to be constantly referred to and where it is not necessary to be

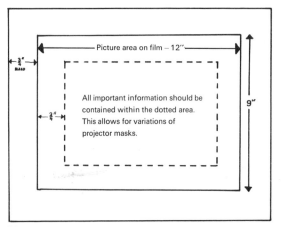

26.
Preparation of artwork for filmstrip, i.e. single frames 18mm × 24mm.
Artwork for slides (double frames, 24mm × 36mm) will be in proportion 2 : 3 with equivalent allowance for bleed and for variations of projector frame.

able to make direct visual comparisons between frames (possible with overhead projector).

Slides or filmstrip linked with audio tape:
It is far easier and cheaper to make a good job of a slide-tape sequence than of a TV production or of a cineloop.

It is also easier to change and adapt, teachers are less likely to hang on to outdated material due to the low original costs.

Stills, particularly slides, have better colour and definition than both film and television. If motion is not absolutely necessary, why use it?

Observations on Design and Production

The content of each frame should be kept to a minimum. A teacher reviewing a filmstrip said, 'The frame was so full, it needed 15 minutes projection time and burnt up. It should have been a wallchart!'

No colour photographic processes match the

original photograph print or artwork exactly. Some colours are degraded more than others, pastel colours lose strength and go to gray. Blues tend to become darker and yellows lighter; magentas and purples become reddish; greens and cyans bluish. These tendencies may be partly corrected by colour filters. However, in filmstrips a mean must be established for all frames as they are printed as one unit.

By use of colour filter black lettering on white can appear as white on colour, e.g. producing the complementary to the filter colour.

Dayglo pigments produce excellent blues, greens and magentas.

Glare from the screen producing eye fatigue may be reduced by avoiding too much contrast between frames. Generally, a dark colour (a deep blue is very satisfactory) with the information - lettering, graphs, etc. - in white, is less fatiguing than black information on a pale background.

Artwork should be 9 in. x 12 in. for filmstrip, 10 in. x 15 in. for slides. (or in those proportions) with generous bleed for camera. Keep important material well within the above areas, as some projectors have peculiar masks and vital parts may not be projected. (Fig. 26)

The size of artwork lettering and detail depends on the size of projected image and the maximum viewing distance expected (See *Legibility Part 3*)

For slide-audio tape linked material it is important for the subject writers to realize that the attention will be primarily on the visual. Mc G. Harden of the Department of Medicine in Glasgow, who has worked on this method, says it is better to prepare the visual material first of all, then to compose the script while looking at the slides.

27.
The reaction of children looking at a film.

FILM

Description

Variations of projected image sizes:

Cinema size and Panavision, 3-D, etc. average size 18 ft x 16 ft

Lecture hall maximum size 10 ft x 8 ft

Classroom (slides and 16mm) maximum size 50 in. x 50 in.

Rear projection   maximum size 25 in. x 19 in.

Cineloop   maximum size 18 in. x 12 in.

The three gauges of film used in education are 8mm, 16mm and 35mm. 8mm film is usually reserved for short films of 4 to 8 minutes in length; 16mm and 35mm for films of 15 minutes and over.

Other points of difference between 8mm, 16mm and 35mm films are their associated image sizes and definition; smaller and poorer for the 8mm.

The most significant development in film for education in recent years is the 8mm loop film usually lasting 4 to 6 minutes. It is sold in a cassette and is selfthreading. A special projector, often incorporating a rear projection screen, is required.

200,000 projectors were in use in the USA in 1968, 7500 in Great Britain.

One blemish on the rosy future of the 8mm loop film is the controversy over whether Super 8 or Standard 8 should be used. Super 8 produces a 20 per cent bigger image with increased definition. However, Standard 8 is cheaper and well established. If only the two types could be used on the same projector, there would then be no problem. Unfortunately, this is not so, and many potential buyers are waiting to see which will become predominant.

Both types are produced commercially and are shot on 16mm or 35mm film and copied.

A new challenge to 8mm loop film is coming from the development of EVR (Electronic Video Recording, a television videotape in cassette form).

Both media lend themselves to almost identical aims, objectives and teaching/learning steps, and as they will both be equally cheap it will be interesting to see if one ousts the other. A massive choice of 8mm loop films already exists which is essential for teachers. On the other hand, EVR is transmitted by the standard television receiver, which is becoming increasingly common in most American and West European schools as well as many poorer countries.

A very important factor is that both 8mm loop film and EVR can be stopped at any frame. Another recent development is the multi screen movie. A number of films or films and slides can be shown at the same time. It is claimed that this is a medium particularly well suited to establishing relationships between concepts.

There is still little evidence of its use in education. Considering the results of research into perception concerning the amount of data the mind can handle, it may be doubted whether the multi-screen movie has any wide application. But who knows, it is just this type of idea which might prove to be an exhilarating and fresh answer to a particular teaching/learning sequence.

Characteristics and Teaching Use

Film is highly motivational.

Film can provide the nearest substitute for life experience, having the possibility of realistic image, colour, movement, time and sound.

However, film is not life and thereby gains for

learning as much as it loses, ie. one can be selective and order the subject for greater comprehensibility and for dramatic impact.

Several Teaching/Learning Steps can be served by a single film, from general presentation of a new subject, to a real life selected example, to diagrammatic analysis and the introduction of a general concept. A very useful characteristic of film is the possibility it presents of relating symbol to reality.

In terms of subject matter films make possible experiences which would be geographically impossible or financially prohibitive. Famous people, dangerous experiments, tiny phenomena, long time phenomena can all be brought to the learner as near life-like experiences.

The range of visual techniques is great, allowing many ways of communicating for different objectives, different learning steps and different viewers. Microphoto, telephoto, animation, overprinting, time lapse, slow motion and stop motion combined with zoom, fade and mix make a formidable armoury.

The possibility of camera movement make the solidity and spatial relationship of the environment more 'graspable'. A camera moving towards and around a piece of sculpture or over a landscape gives an understanding of the third dimension.

Moving film has a life quality which is contrasted with stills from films which are peculiarly unreal.

Long films

Long films can give a rich and varied introduction to a new subject. Short films are more suitable for the follow-up of specific points.

Long films tend to be 'polyvalent', i.e. to have a number of aims, uses and types of audience in mind.

This variety of visual experience may be suitable not only for the general introduction to a subject, but for the time when the teacher wants the students to be plunged deliberately into a mass of information, from which they must work out a system and a sense.

However, all too often the long film is too crowded and confusing. It is difficult to fit it into a particular learning sequence devised for particular viewers.

8mm loop films

8mm loop films average 4 minutes in length. They usually deal with a single concept, demonstration or topic.

Technically, they are immediately available.

Any frame may be held by remote control.

Their adaptability means that they may easily be fitted into individually devised Teaching/Learning Sequences.

The special contribution of 8mm loop film lies in the possibilty of analysing a concept and, in particular, of analysing a limited real life situation and relating it to the symbology of the concept, for example, a formula can be built up by the overprinting of a live action film of a scientific process.

The sciences, geography, engineering, sport and skill training are all likely to benefit from the short, analytical approach of the 8mm loop film.

Observations on Design and Production

It is not possible to describe film making in this book, eg. camera angles, lighting, story board principle, etc. (see further reading). However, educational film production is often not specifically dealt with. Particularly in 8mm short film production certain points should be considered:

Firstly, the subject matter to be covered and the teaching approach intended should be closely analysed and ideally be written down in small steps.

A short film is very short! It is a problem to combine, in only a few minutes, live action film, animation, overprinting and other techniques and retain clarity of theme and meaning.

An unfamiliar viewpoint, bit of film technique or a strange word might catch and hold the attention. The subsequent sequence will be lost and so may be the point of the film. One must adjust the technical presentation to suit the particular learner intended.

Motivation in short films is far less important than clarity of image and sequence. It is better to use special effects only for directing and controlling attention. 8mm short film is not mini 16mm, no dramatic build-up is required. Titles are unnecessary except possibly to mark the beginning of a sequence.

Present the ideas at a pace that the intended learner can take.

The relationship between the diagrammatic analysis or the close-up shot and the total view may become lost, unless the film continually relates back to the known aspect.

It is quite possible for the film to become just a fantasy of shapes and colours to the viewer if this continual linking with the known aspect does not take place.

Animation often encourages this slipping into a fantasy world. The style of representation and movement in animation can become so characterful that the viewer may think the subject is actually like that, rather than seeing it as just a visual metaphor.

Similarly, there is a danger in the compression of time by time lapse photography, it can give a false impression. A time lapse study of a well known flower will not deceive people into thinking that some types of flower go from bud to pod in two minutes flat. However, a piece of time lapse film of an unfamiliar object may be a stronger experience than the object itself and leave the viewer with the feeling that it does its evolution cycle in an unenviably short time! This is a serious danger. However, if the designer could include familiar or easily understandable information in the sequences before and after the time lapse sequence, and includes perhaps a clock, it might be overcome.

When changing from natural action to slow motion and back again, the same camera position or viewpoint should be kept.

In filming movement it must be clear whether it is the object which is moving or the camera; with unknown objects or aspects this may not be self-evident.

Stopframe sequences are often used, for example, in sports films. This is a useful technique if the length of time that each picture is arrested for is long enough for the mind to take it in.

For films dealing with manual skills it is important to give the viewpoint of the learner doing the job himself, ie. film over the typist's shoulder rather than from the side.

Scale must be established.

Although the artwork is filmed on 16mm or 35 mm gauge, it is often forgotten that the distributed prints are only 8mm copies.

Definition on 8mm loop film is often poor and frames stopped by the remote control tend to go out of focus.

Details, eg. formulae, are sometimes not readable. Use considerably larger type than that

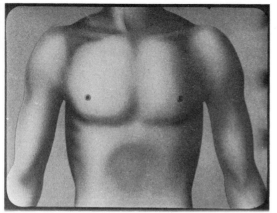

28

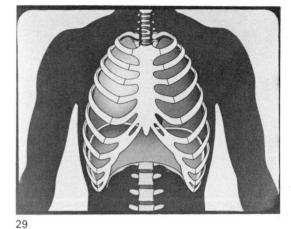

29

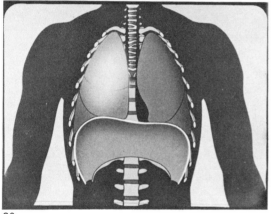

30

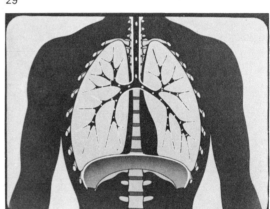

31

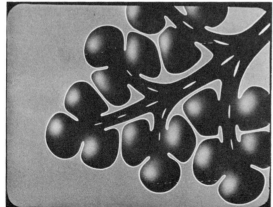

32

28-32.
'Breathing'. Stills from a 8mm cineloop.

This film never loses the learner. He is taken from what he knows through clearly linked aspects to the lung bud and back again along the same path. The images depend more on tonal contrast than on colour, compensating for the poor definition of 8mm film.

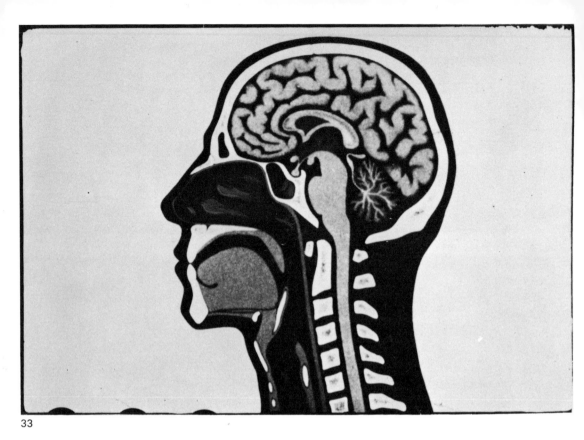

33

34

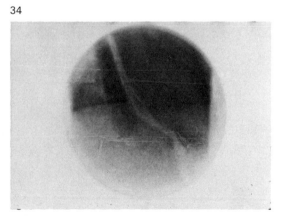

'Swallowing'. Slides from a 8mm cineloop. Animation and X-ray film. The depiction of brain etc. is an irrelevancy and a distraction.

Fig. 34 is an X-ray film still of someone swallowing. The loop is a combination of live actionfilm and animation. The animation is tonally bold and simple, essential for 8mm loop film.

Fig. 35 is a suggested amendment.

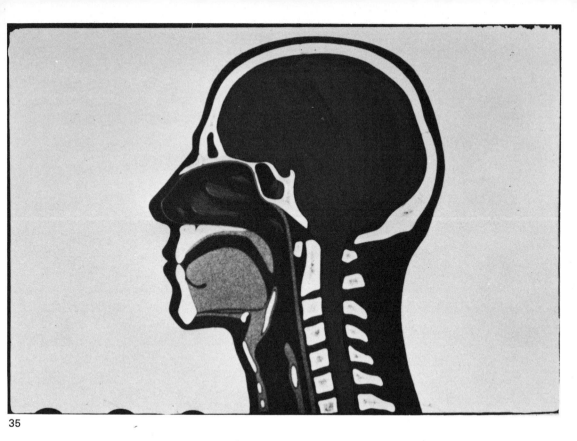

35

suggested in Part 3, *Legibility* section, which is based on sharply defined print and good contrast.

Similarly, use close-up and middle close-up more often than for conventional filming.

Colours tend to become pastelly. To differentiate important areas use bright colours and strong tonal contrasts whenever possible.

Titles: only use titles and labelling when it is absolutely necessary, thereby giving the teacher the possibility to supply them as he wishes.

Another important reason for this is that 8mm loop films are increasingly sold internationally. Preferably use only markers and arrows, etc. Leave any titles on for longer than the time normally required to read that length.

If there is a sound track, do not pack it (See *Word and Picture, Part 3*).

To summarize: The learner will **know less** about the subject than the designer/film maker and must be looked after!

37

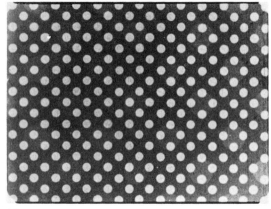

38

'Surface Tension'. 16mm film.

36-41
The learner is taken from the example of surface tension with which he is familiar, through the analysis of the basic concept and back again to examples of the phenomenon in life. The film achieves, with great success, the relation between life examples and symbolic analysis. There is some scale discrepancy in showing the molecules as a pattern within the tumbler. This mixed-scale convention could create the wrong impression about the size of the molecules.

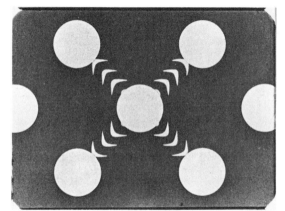

39
40

41. A coin floating on the miniscus.

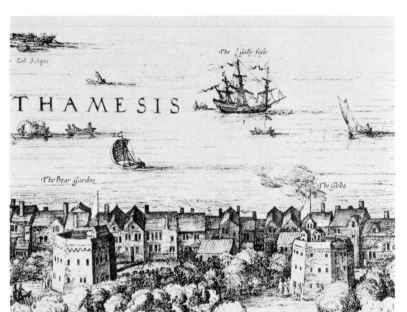

42

Shakespeare theatre.

42-45
Old prints, artist's reconstruction drawings, models and live demonstrations are some of the visual means of presentation possible in television.

43

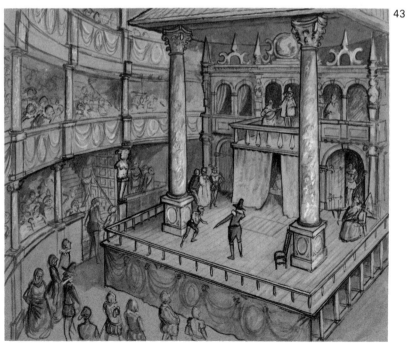

TELEVISION

Description

In educational use screen sizes vary from 21 in. to 27 in. Some are larger.

National and regional television networks broadcast educational programmes.

Educational Closed Circuit Television (ECCTV) is established in Great Britain by the City Education Authorities of Glasgow, Plymouth, London; in universities, training colleges and a few schools. ECCTV is widely established and highly developed in the US at regional and local level, the Ford Foundation alone spends over $100 million on educational television.

Videotape is a sound and vision recording similar to audio tape. It can be used quickly and easily. It can be wound and rewound at speed to the required part. One can freeze any frame; no processing is required.

It is used in CCTV set-ups, cost precludes its use for the individual classroom.

EVR (Electronic Video Recording) provides low cost recording of television programmes. Sold in a cassette it can be transmitted by an adapted television set. It plays instantly and can be stopped at any frame without loss of quality.

Full commercial production is expected by the mid 1970s. Being cheaper and easier to use than videotape it could become well established, providing a big enough selection can be built up quickly.

Characteristics and Teaching Use

Television contacts mass audiences and gives the possibility of mass teaching. In economic terms, this is important, e.g. in a Mexican anti illiteracy campaign one and a half million people are said to have been 'educated'. Poorer countries frequently decide to invest capital in television centres rather than in more traditional teaching methods.

However, the preparation of programmes for mass audiences has disadvantages:

a) the time of the broadcasts may be inconvenient;

b) there is no possibility of adjusting the content and presentation to particular groups of learners;

c) communication is one way, there is no possibility for pupil interaction with the programme.

ECCTV to some degree overcomes these drawbacks. However, it is still not fully adaptable to the situation of specific classes or individuals. EVR is the most flexible and adaptable form of television. Being in a cassette it can be used at just the moment required and only that section which the teacher wants the students to see need be shown.

More recent developments include the possibilities of students' interaction with the visual material displayed on the cathode ray tube.

A fully equipped television studio offers many technical possibilities and devices, for example, live demonstration, live action film, animation, models, graphics, photomotion and magnification.

Compared with film, superimposition, fade-outs and dissolves are all easier to do by television. Further, live demonstration on television is always more convincing than in a film.

These characteristics of television make the whole range of visual representation possible, from naturalism to abstract statements.

Teachers still widely classify television as being most useful for a stimulating presentation of a new subject or for general enrichment. However, there is more to it than this.

Television lends itself not only to presentation in the Teaching/Learning sequence, but to analysis and synthesis, the visual unfolding of arguments, displaying the evidence, guiding observation and sorting out possibilities.

Television can assist in the learning of skills, in the changing of attitudes and towards the development of appreciation, as well as in the gathering of facts and towards the understanding of concepts.

Observations on Design and Production

For standard television graphics practice, see Roy Laughton, *TV Graphics*, (Studio Vista and Reinhold).

One of the first considerations when working for educational television will be ease of readability (see Part 3). Viewers may be 24 ft away from the screen. Taking into account the low definition of the television screen and allowing for poor receivers, lettering must have a body height of 3/4 in. on the screen as a minimum, if this viewing distance is likely.

In educational television there is often the temptation, particularly in economy run CCTV, to use material not specifically prepared for television, e.g. books and charts. It is essential here to ensure that the tones are not too contrasty, and, on the other hand, that the visual is not too dependent on nuances of tone which will not show up. Ideally, too, material should be centred with good margins. Type faces appropriate for books may not work on television. (See *Legibility Part 3*)

The use of the still is of great importance in educational television. It is cheaper and simpler to produce than film. It is highly economical in that it can be designed exactly to requirements, avoiding costs of processing and editing. Movement is not always essential and quite often a still is positively required, particularly where observation of content detail is necessary.

Diagrams should be kept very simple, remembering television definition. It is recommended that a basic grey with a 25 per cent light reflectance be used. Grid and reference lines can be white, numbers and data lines in black. Also note, that horizontal lines, if too narrow, will be 'lost' in the horizontal lines of the screen.

Colour television will, no doubt, become universal, however, for some time, coloured captions, diagrams, models and sets will be transmitted in black and white and must rely on clear tonal differences. These, of course, will be tried out on the monitor at an early stage.

Photographs should be kept as simple and in as clearly defineable shape divisions as possible. If necessary, spray down confusing detail. Contrasty, crisp photos tend to appear as black and white on the receiver; photos made of the middle greys tend to show better. Use matt rather than gloss paper.

2 in. x 2 in. slides (telops or telecine slides) are commonly used for television. They should be double frame and horizontal.

The overhead projector is also a useful tool, so is technamation.

Simple animation can be achieved through camera movement, zooming, panning, cutting, etc. Ensure that the camera, in moving about the still, does not pick up corners and edges of unwanted material.

Pointers, labels, arrows, underlinings, circling and contrasting tones can be used to direct

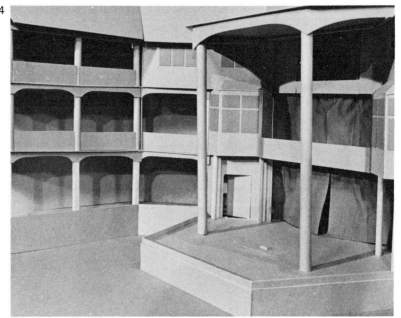

46

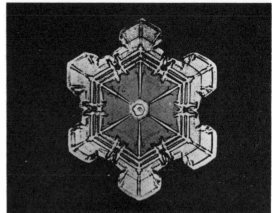

47

48

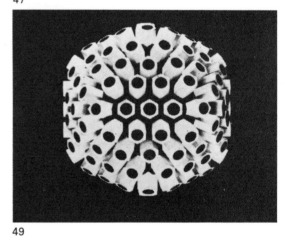

49

46-50

The characteristics of television make the whole range of visual presentation possible. In a programme on symmetry, photographic enlargements of snow flakes and microphotos of a virus, models, diagrams and live demonstration by magnet board were used to present some of the concepts.

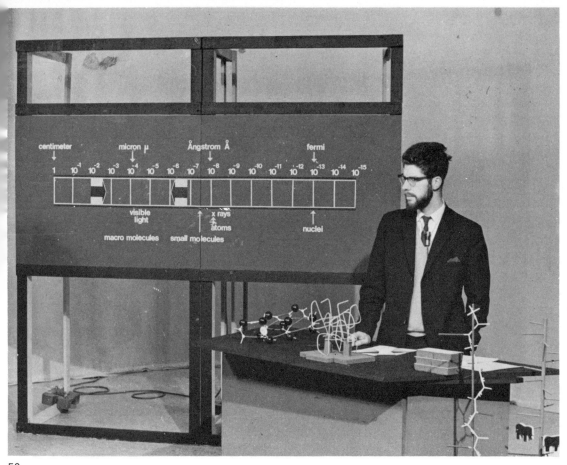

50

attention. When the attention must be more rigorously controlled the information can be built up, bit by bit, on a magnet board or flannelboard or revealed by simple slide animation. When text is shown, it should relate meaningfully and usually exactly to the spoken commentary or complete distraction may result. Try to make the words appear at the moment they are wanted by strip animation, the use of two cameras, etc.

The work of the designer in educational television, particularly if in a CCTV set-up, will be a bit of a 'Jack of all trades'. He can, incidentally, become a person of central importance in a small set-up, sometimes working directly with subject specialists to the practical exclusion of producers.

51

52.
Television 'Mrs Gaskell, the nineteenth-century writer and author of *Cranford* visits Manchester'. Drawing designed for television camera movement. The four rectangles indicate areas over which the camera will pan.

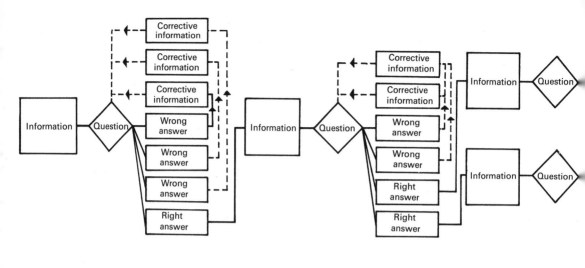

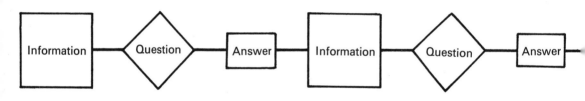

53-54. Programmed Learning: Linear and adaptive or branching.

PROGRAMMED LEARNING AND TEACHING MACHINES

Description

A programme takes the place of the teacher and leads the learner through a series of statements and questions which he must answer. The sequence is so planned that his understanding and knowledge grows at each step until the final objective is reached.

The steps, which are actually separate frames appearing on the machine (or in the book) are very gradual so that the questions are almost certain to be answered correctly.

The good feature of Programmed Learning is that the learner has to participate and interact with the material to go forward (contrast reading a book, watching a film or just sitting in class).

There are two main types of Programmed Learning, 'linear' and 'adaptive'. In linear Programmed Learning (Fig. 53) the learner goes along a fixed sequence of steps like stepping stones. He can sometimes go back to check but that is all.

In adaptive Programmed Learning (Fig. 54) there are a great number of ways through to the goal. The programme has, to greater or lesser extent, the possibility of being adapted to the learner's particular answer. In linear Programmed Learning there was only one answer possible. In adaptive Programmed Learning there is a choice. If you choose a wrong answer you are directed through a series of 'corrective training' steps before carrying on. Though, as with the divisions in a family tree, there is a limit to the amount of special corrective steps possible.

One thing is quite clear about these two types of Programmed Learning: linear is easier to produce. The machine need only be very simple. Indeed, a book of Programmed Learning may be just as satisfactory as a machine. (See Fig.55) Adaptive programming can be as complicated as the machine can handle and the authors devise. A relatively limited adaptive machine would be, for example, the ITM Grundytutor. (See Fig. 56)

The extreme in adaptive machinery is the computer with its associated devices of electronically connected typewriters and cathode ray tube display screens. (See Figs 57, 58)

The marriage between Programmed Learning as an educational method and modern machinery is a tremendous potential for self instruction. A computer can adapt to as many learner differences as the course writers can compose alternations for.

One of the most impressive uses of a computer is in the University of Illinois, where the PLATO experiment has a potential capacity of 5000 student terminals.

There is far more to Programmed Learning and Teaching Machines than mentioned here (see further reading, which also mentions designer's use of computers).

Prospects for the use of the computer

It has been estimated that by 1977 30 per cent of Primary Schools and 50 percent of Secondary Schools in the USA will be using computers. In Great Britain, the use of the computer in schools will not be widespread until the 1980s. However, many universities and industries already have computers and there is increasing interest in their use for education.

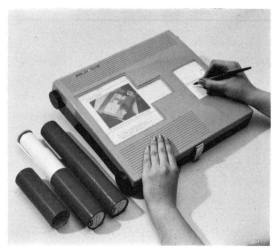

55
A simple linear programme machine, the Bingley Tutor.

56
A machine for branching programmes, the Grundytutor.

An expensive way of learning to read!
The child receives taped instructions from the teacher by earphone; the IBM terminal presents words on the CRT and a rear projection image. The child must touch the correct word on the screen with the light pen, at Stanford Universities Laboratory for Learning.
57

An example of a dubious piece of design for the new technological age.
The designer may look forward in the future to consultation and design of images to be displayed by the CRT, both computer generated and the more traditional type, computer controlled.
58

Visuals associated with Teaching Machines

The manually operated machines are often simply rolls of paper, usually printed in line only.

Rear projection machines may use slides, filmstrip, microfilm- microfiche, also film or videotape for the programmed frames.

Computers can either control the projection of all the above conventional visuals or generate pictures through a cathode ray tube.

Characteristics and Teaching Use

To summarize:

1. Programmed Learning is a form of self instruction demanding active participation.
2. Programmed Learning adapts to individual needs as far as the associated machinery permits.
3. Programmed Learning is a suitable approach to subjects which lend themselves to an analytical presentation, particularly where there can be right and wrong answers.
4. Appreciation and attitudes are less likely objectives for Programmed Learning than knowledge, factually based concepts and skills.

Observations on Design and Production

Where conventional aids are used the reader is referred to the appropriate section in this book.

However, three comments may be made:

Although the images are seen at close quarters, there is the disadvantage that rear projection tends to lack contrast and indeed can be fuzzy and pock-marked if enlarged from microfilm. Allow for this, therefore, in spite of close range use.

Secondly, Programmed Learning is essentially self instruction, i.e. there will be no pointing finger on the visual display to control the learner's attention. The visual display must, therefore, assist this self instruction by visual control of attention.

Thirdly, the intensity of working in a hooded self instructional booth can be relieved and rewarded through the visuals, character and quality.

Summary and Prospects for the Artist

McLuhan (*The Medium is the Massage*) is right in the sense that the possibilities of Computer Aided Learning are so rich that the whole concept of learning and teaching and indeed some aims of education, could be changed to fit the medium. The experienced and visually thinking person can play a big part in this, in the very origination of programmes.

Kenneth C. Knowlton of Bell Telephones - a leading man in the computer field - said,

'we need to develop a great deal of collaboration between artists and programmers in order to develop meaningful, understandable and useful sets of tools and ways of using them.'

This book can do no more than to direct the reader to this important sphere.

WALLCHARTS, WALLPOSTERS, WALLPICTURES

Description
Wallcharts vary from 39 in. x 40 in. to 40 in. x 60 in. in size;

Wallposters and wallpictures vary form 15 in. x 20 in. to 20 in. x 30 in.

All three media are usually printed by lithography in several colours.

Wallcharts are frequently expected to convey a concept in both abstract terms and by the illustration of examples. One chart may be photograph, artist drawing, symbol, graph and words.

Wallposters usually attempt to convey only a limited piece of information.

Wallpictures present a naturalistic representation by an artist or photographer.

Both posters and pictures tend to be for propaganda, e.g. health, safety, etc.

Characteristics and Teaching Use:
All three media, though very different in some ways, share the following characteristics:

they are static and relatively small, compared with projected images. However, they are bigger than most rear projection images and gain by having better definition.

The content is predetermined by the producer, making adaptability, especially of the complicated chart, a problem.

Wallcharts:
Producers of wallcharts are traditionally given a sharp rap over the knuckles by writers on audio-visual materials. The main criticism levelled is that far too much information is put into the charts, making them confusing and often physically impossible to read from halfway down the classroom. It is felt by some audio-visual specialists that the wallchart has even become totally redundant in face of other developments, both in material and methods. Yet, there is something undeniably useful about being able to summarize an idea on a single visual for semi-permanent display.

Further, there is no reason why a wallchart should not carry a lot of information if it is to be used for small group work only.

In terms of the Teaching/Learning Sequence a wallchart is most likely to be used to summarize points already learnt in other ways. It will be useful as a mnemonic (reminder), as an encyclopedic display of information for future reference.

In terms of objectives, wallcharts are useful as a reference summary of stages in a manual skill, particularly if the skill has already been introduced by other means. The chart can be on permanent or semi-permanent display, e.g. First Aid, the kiss of life method.

The designer must isolate the main stages, select the viewpoint which is not only clear but with which an onlooker can identify. He must design a connected sequence in which those parts not shown are nevertheless understood.

Facts, rather than a general concept, is another valid objective for the wallchart. Here, the large area of the chart can display a great number of visual bits of information for reference, for example, various types of plant.

The designer should concentrate on making any comparison, which might be made by the learner, as easy as possible. The chart must be designed so that the learner's eye can scan over a variety of other bits of information without being distracted.

Particularly when the chart contains a mass of information, unnecessary detail should never be given and this might include colour and texture. For example, in a chart designed to enable comparisons to be made between plants it may be a total and distracting irrelevancy to show colour.

Concepts are the most useful objective for charts. There is no reason why charts with this objective need not be successful if the criteria of Part I are recognised by the producer and by the teacher who uses the chart. But so often this does not happen.

Are the particular learners intended to be able to link the various bits of information and see a basic theme? Very often it is only possible to see a basic principle in a chart if one is already familiar with the concept.

The relating of information, reading graphs and drawing conclusions, as stated in Part I, is a doubtful and unreliable ability in young people or people of any age who are not used to it. Unfortunately, it is precisely these people who are most frequently given charts.

What can the designer do to help?

Principally, he must establish with the subject writer the order in which it is hoped that the viewer will look at the information. It is not enough to establish the sequence with arrows, but the designer must use tonal order, colour emphasis, dynamism of shape, etc. (see Part 3).

Make the main visual path so clear that the viewer will see it immediately and will be able to turn back to it at any time.

When a firm visual order is established, it is possible for the eye to rest at any point without distraction. On the majority of concept charts, however, the eye is flicked from side to side by competing visual elements.

Wallposters lend themselves to the modifying of attitudes. A situation is shown from which the learner must draw a conclusion. A few words may help him. The best words may well not state the conclusion but add another aspect of information to the visual, helping the learner to draw a richer meaning. For example, a poster of a girl who has been knocked down with the words 'A drink for the road'.

Posters need something of the dynamism and singleness of impact which is achieved in advertising.

Wallpictures, by presenting a 'real' if still representation of a topic are also useful at the presentation stage of a Teaching/Learning Sequence.

Wall pictures may not only carry a lot of facts but carry implications which help the objective of Appreciation; for example, a picture of an early 19th-century railway station may make one appreciate the rigours of travel as well as the extreme differences between rich and poor at that time.

Observations on Design and Production

Comments on the design of charts, posters and pictures have been made in each subsection. For further information on readability, symbol, colour and other visual elements vital to these categories of material, see Part 3.

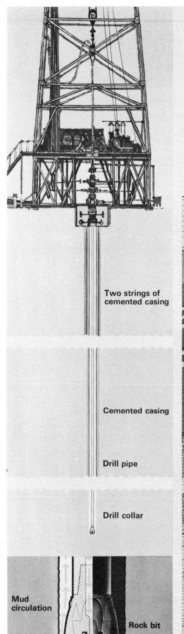

Two strings of
cemented casing

Cemented casing

Drill pipe

Drill collar

Mud
circulation

Rock bit

Drilling and Production

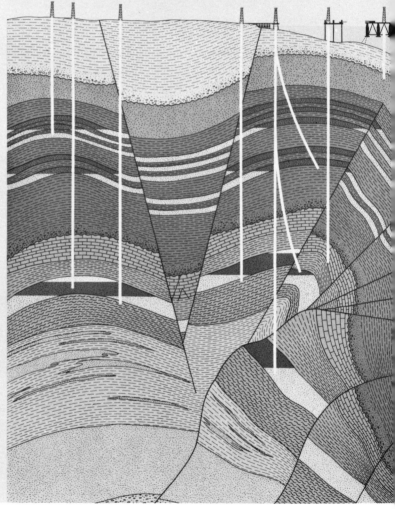

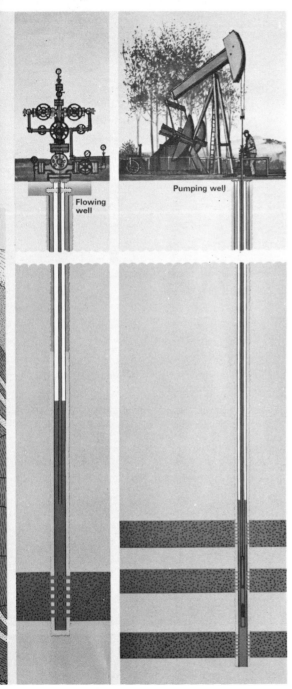

Flowing
well

Pumping well

59.
A clearly organized wallchart, summarizing aspects of
the drilling and production of oil.

MAGNETBOARD, FLANNELBOARD, HOOK AND LOOP BOARD

Description

All three devices act as supports for the display of pictures or single cut out figures or objects. Educational suppliers distribute both the supports and the sheets of drawn objects.

The supports are:

a) Magnetboard: a sheet of tinplate, usually painted;

b) Flannelboard: a brushed nylon sheet;

c) Hook and Loop (or Teazlegraph): a nylon sheet composed of tiny loops of nylon.

The cut out pictures adhere to either the Magnetboard by thin magnets taped on the back, to the Flannelboard by adhesive felt, or the Hook and Loop nylon sheet by very small hooks.

Characteristics and Teaching Use

All three media are cheap to make and to buy. Hence, they are widely used everywhere, especially in poorer countries. They are very dynamic aids for little money and no technical resources.

These media are essentially for use with the demonstrative method of teaching. By controlling the display, the learner's attention can be directed to specific points.

The media are particularly useful in building up, in visual terms, principal factors of a concept, e.g. an industrial process or an economic theory. (Figs 61-63)

This is especially true when the necessary visuals are too complicated to be created on the spot and when there is a dramatic advantage in the flexibility of their handling.

These media may also provide a basis for a limited presentation of life like situations in, for example, the early stages of language teaching. The particular quality of the Magnetboard is that the board itself can be drawn on by the teacher or pupil.

Cut out figures and objects may thus be joined dynamically by the teacher's chalk drawing. This can heighten dramatic impact.

All three media are used in television production when the above qualities are required.

Observations on Design and Production

Each image is a cut out, separate thing. Its outside silhouette will be very important. It is usually fatal to make the object part of a little scene, as this makes the outside shape arbitrary and not easy to interpret from a distance.

As cut out figures are used for group demonstration purposes they must be visible and easy to identify at a viewing distance of 30ft or more.

Screen printing is used to give bright, 'carrying' colours and the possibility of having heavy card. However, if there is to be a long run it should be remembered that ten sheet card can be used with lithography.

60.
Magnetboard. Teaching English to immigrant children.
An inexpensive and highly adaptable aid, giving control
of attention and the possibilities of student involvement.

BOOKS

Books are still the most used visual material for instruction, for example, just under half of the money spent on instructional materials in the USA is on books.

The range of types of books is great; textbooks, encyclopedias, programmed learning books, workbooks, magazines, instruction cards and numerous subdivisions of each category.

The variety of books and associated design problems is enormous and any attempt at a comprehensive review is beyond the scope of this book and this writer's capability. At the same time, one can assume that book design is a basic component of all designers' training. Two observations only are put forward.

Firstly, the whole nature of the book lends itself

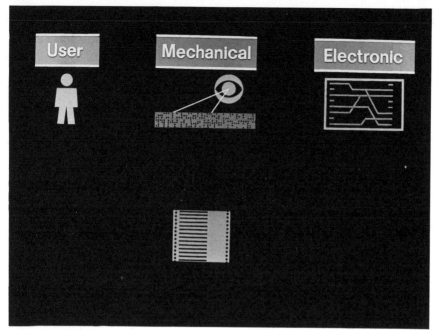

61.
Magnetboard used in television demonstration. Magnetboard used for concept analysis calls for much ruminat-
ing on the part of the designer. He must be able to
simplify complex abstract concepts in visual symbols
which will be recognizable to the learner. The pictograph type of representation is the most useful one.

to individual instruction. As with all self instructional material there may be nothing
between the designer and the learner, no
teacher's directing finger or helpful comment.
The responsibility for bringing about learning
may thus rest on the designer's decisions;
attractive and clear layout will help motivation:
unambiguous and logical layout, the development of the argument.

The second observation relates to the complete
relevance of the designer's work to the instructional objective, the particular learner and learning environment.

'Relevance' is, of course, normally part of a
designer's basic way of thinking. But often the
subject writers do not fully inform the designer
of all that is going on.

An optimum contribution can only be made by
a designer if he has thoroughly understood the
specific use the book is to be put to and how it
fits in with other material.

Thus, if he is not told, he must find out.

62

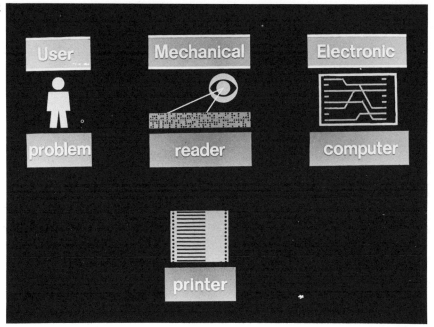

63

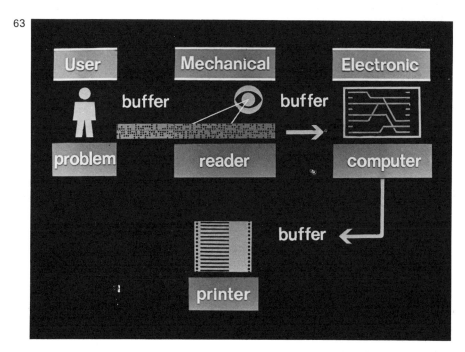

PART 3

Part 3 is concerned with the design of educational visual materials, with the following two criteria as a basis;

first, the visual must be so designed that the learner can physically see it and recognise its content;

secondly, the design of the material must take into account the learner's interpretation of and response to what he sees.

PERCEPTION

Forty people travelling in a coach through a town will see forty different sets of things. If a guide points to a particular feature there may still be forty different reactions to it and aspects of it observed. Each person will interpret according to his personality, experience, preoccupation or whim of the moment.

This variety of interpretation must be expected with educational visual materials as well. However, the difference between the town, a real life context, and visual communication is that the latter is the result of selective presentation. This selection will attempt to control what people perceive by limiting what they are given. The selection will be the specific qualities of the object or the idea we want the learner to receive.

In visual terms, these qualities will be shown by the elements of shape, form, colour, etc. and by symbols which together represent an idea. The design of educational visual materials is concerned not only with clarity but with dynamic emphasis on the important visual elements and relationships so that greater significance and meaning may be given to the subject. These two qualities of clarity and of dynamic

expression will provide the basis for the remaining sections.

SHAPE AND COMPOSITION

The identity and character of a shape depends on its 'structural skeleton'. Our awareness of this structure results firstly from the movement of the eye round the edge of the shape, and secondly across it, in certain specific directions peculiar to the individual shape. (Fig. 67)

Although shape must be defined and made visible by lines, tones, colours, etc, it is a definable quality in its own right and as such provides the main characteristic by which an object can be recognized.

Characterful and identifiable shape is given pride of place over other visual elements by both psychologists of perception and by art historians.

Particularly important is the relationship of shapes within some kind of frame, i.e. composition.

Clarity, Recognition, Expression

Figures 64 and 65 are wall posters, 15 in. x 21 in, designed to be used with a maximum viewing distance of 30 ft. They are from a series of 120 designed for language teaching. The very simple, clearly differentiated shapes are easy to see and distinguish (clarity); the basic shape differences between the two boys make them easy to recognize and to differentiate and this also applies when the two boys are depicted on a far smaller scale elsewhere (recognition).

The background shapes are not arbitrary decorative features but are intended to express some

64. Wallposters for language teaching.
Shape used for clarity, ease of recognition and character-ful impact.

65

67. Drawings after Arnheim.

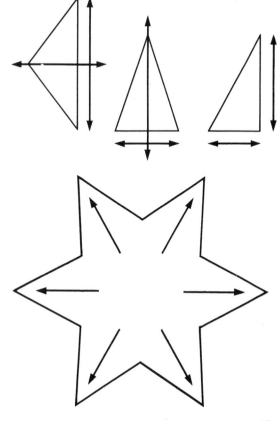

66.
Friendly characters, but distinguishable only by their 'feature tags'; adequate as pictographs for use at close quarters and when a semi-symbol is required, rather than a 'real life' representation (see also Figs 89-96).

of the character of the two boys (expression). The other drawings (Fig. 66) do not have memorable or easily identifiable shape and rely on 'tags', eg. hair quiffs, for recognition. It would be difficult to recognize and distinguish these four faces at a distance.

Their shape and line are in no way expressive.

Clarity

Simplicity of individual shapes and of the main groupings of shape is important for clarity and for ease and speed of recognition. Particularly in the case of charts or book pages, when a large

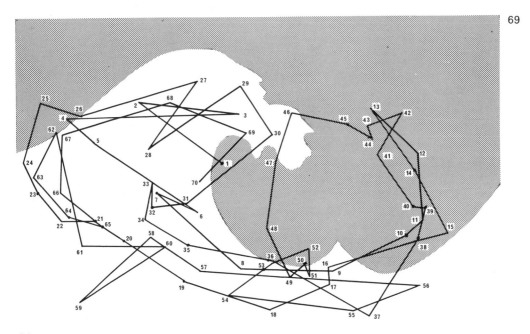

amount of information must be presented at one time, an overall structure which clearly defines the place and function of every detail is essential.

Children particularly, as mentioned before (Part 1, Learner, Age) have difficulty in distinguishing a main theme from a mass of detail. They must be very firmly guided to see basic relationships.

The attention can be directed around a visual by many methods known to artists. The directional properties of shape are shown here by the plottings of eye movement on a Hokusai drawing (Figs 68, 69)

In a composition, visual elements of similar quality are seen as belonging together, thus directing attention and creating relationships (Principle of Similarity).

Controlling the movement and attention of the viewer's eye is obviously a critical factor in visual communication. It would be interesting and very worthwhile to make eye attention tracings of various types and ages of people to specific visuals intended for instructional purposes.

Figure-Ground

Broadly, this is a term given by psychologists to the relationship of an object depicted and its background. The two are often confused; which is background, which is object?

The drawings devised by psychologists to prove this difficulty of perception must be well known to artists. However, this is not just a joke-trick irrelevancy. With the best will in the world an artist can intend one thing, but other people may see it quite differently.

Diagrams, simplified drawings and maps may all lead to misinterpretations.

The designer must not assume that other people will see it his way and must provide adequate cues for unmistakable interpretation. Objects seen against complicated backgrounds may also 'join up' and be lost. Although clarity and characterful unity of shape will help identification, form, solidity, texture and space may have to be developed to detach the object from its background.

Recognition

The need to recognize recurring objects and symbols is a basic factor in using educational visual materials.

Characterful and memorable shape will contribute much to this. Other cues given, for example by colour or by 'tags' will be useful extras when the object is less known or presented from a strange viewpoint.

Expression

Clarity and ease of recognition are fairly obvious needs. It is, however, much more difficult to discuss the contribution to be made by a dynamic use of visual elements to the expression of meaning.

The shape and composition in the wallposter of George and the worm (Fig. 70) are not only

70. The diagonal thrust of aggression.

easy to distinguish at 30ft but express by the diagonal lunge the language associated with it. It is essential that visual materials for education provide experiences rather than uninteresting and uninvolving occurrances. Even in more abstract visual arrangements this heightened expressiveness of subject matter through shape is vital.

SPACE AND THREE-DIMENSIONAL REPRESENTATION

Maurice George of the United Kingdom Atomic Energy Commission recently described the growing use of three dimensional scaled drawings by the UKEA.

A great amount of engineering thought can be conveyed visually so that the features and functions can be clearly understood without the use of purely technical information.

'Constructors find them invaluable in placing components, in the same way that chemical engineers use models for complex pipework for which engineering drawings would be too confusing.'

If three dimensional representation is useful at this level for technically skilled audiences, then how much more so it must be for the less experienced.

A three dimensional statement is particularly necessary when complex objects are unfamiliar. Two dimensional representations may be very abstract and should only be used when the various lines and shapes can be related to clearly understood previous experience.

A three dimensional representation also contributes to a sense of presence and reality and this may be necessary when the intention is to grip and convince the viewer in some way. A sense of solidity also gives the object more

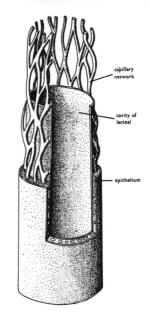

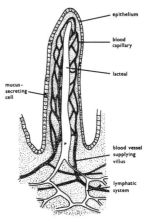

71.
Book illustration. Villus structure. Does the two- or three-dimensional representation provide the more significant information?

identity and helps counteract figure-ground confusion.

There must be many more reasons for representing solidity and space, and many occasions for doing so, yet it is not a method followed, or at least stressed very much, neither in technical drawings nor in illustrations.

It is more difficult to think in three dimensions without visual support, not only for the learner but for the artist, too; it takes longer to execute and often more ability is required - it costs more. Convergence and foreshortening, overlap, shadows, atmospheric perspective, constancy (knowledge of the size of objects), loss of detail in familiar objects, these and other well known methods contribute to the creation of an effect of space and form.

Various types of perspective convey different effects.

Wide angles of divergence are used by architects to give a monumental quality. When a grid is used in which angles of difference are suppressed there is a feeling of proximity. However, the end result of methods used must be to create, first of all, a sense of form and space. The techniques must not be used for their own sake to be left on the surface of the paper as meaningless distractions.

COLOUR

An important aspect of colour is that it costs money to reproduce it. An important question, therefore, is, 'Will colour be really necessary for the task in hand and if so, just what for?' The following categories of colour use might be helpful in making decisions.

Descriptive Use of Colour

Colour adds information. It might help to make an object more recognisable, e.g. colour and tone criteria are standard ways of differentiating similar types of bird.

Where there are weak tonal differences, colour might be essential for recognition.

Some subjects we associate very much with colour and its absence might be odd.

Decorative - Attractive Use of Colour

This is the most common justification produced for having colour. In general, it may be true that colour helps motivation but this cannot be assumed. In fact, research into the use of colour in film has shown repeatedly that it does not affect learning very much.

'People like colour.' This is dangerous as a sole basis for having it. People may not like the colours you like.

21,060 people may have put colours into the following order of preference: blue, red, green, violet, orange and yellow, but they do not really care too much until the colours are used in a particular situation. Yellow margarine is preferred to the more naturally produced green margarine, though green is placed higher up the list. Other factors to consider about these research results are that each colour sample was only one hue and that they were judged in isolation.

To summarize: it cannot be doubted that people, and particularly children, like colour, but if the criterion for choice is the artist's subjective evaluation of what is pleasant, then it cannot be assumed that others will agree. However, if colour is used, first of all, for one of the other purposes listed here, it is far more likely to be acceptable. People may then accept it for its functional value and add pleasure if they feel like it.

Expressive Use of Colour

It is no doubt true and of use to the designer that certain colours may be universally felt to harmonise or clash. What is far less clear is that other, more emotional responses to colours follow any kind of universal. Although research has established that reds activate the nervous system more than greens, it has not come to many other firm conclusions.

People's emotional interpretations are varied: green is taken as peaceful by one person and as representing jealousy by another, but put the same green onto a tree and both would simply see it as foliage.

What I feel is that colour may help to stimulate a particular emotional expression when it is in a context in which other elements are contributing to the same effect.

Diagrammatic Use of Colour

Probably the most significant use of colour is to direct attention and to differentiate areas, particularly when the shapes are complicated. A good case may be seen when comparing the London underground map with and without colour.

Passive combinations and active combinations of colours might be used to direct attention more dynamically than mere colour differences. An interaction between two depicted components might be heightened by using interacting colours.

Symbolic Use of Colour

Brown, blue, green-and-yellow are the new international code colours for electrical wiring. Maps employ a similar, nearly universal coding. As with all symbols, one should check that the particular learner in question will know the code one uses.

For further comments on symbols, see page 82. Currently the sheer cost of colour reproduction in most media enforces some kind of disciplined analysis of whether or not colour is necessary and desirable.

A considerable burden of decision will be put on the artist in the future when colour will be technically and economically easy to reproduce in all media.

The question will still be, however, 'do we want it and why?'

TONE (VALUE)

Controlled tonal relationships within a visual may help clarity and direct attention. Tonal differences make shapes discernible and, on the other hand, similar tones create relationships.

Tonal richness which may occur from small differences of tone has a valuable motivational effect. The tonal weight of bodies of text and pictures in black only may radiate greater richness and quality than if they were in one or two colours.

Tones may also be expressive, the shining light and satanic gloom, depending on their setting, will be interpreted fairly universally.

In the map of Germany designed for the Overhead Projector (Fig. 73) the qualities of clarity, ease of recognition and expression are all there. In terms of expression, the black surrounding area of Europe encloses Germany and makes the arrows and their bursting expansion more meaningful.

72. Book illustration by Maurice Sendak. Expressive use of tone and shape.

73. Overhead projector transparencies. Germany explodes. Tone assists not only clarity and recognition of the shapes but adds to the emotional understanding of the situation.

72

73

Die Schneider mit den Scheren, die kehrten sich herum,
Sie stürzten auf die Alte mit schrecklichem Gebrumm.
„Heraus nun mit dem Gelde! Da hilft kein Ach und Weh!"
Das Mütterlein, das alte, das kreischte: „Ach herrje!"

Ein Geisbock kam geronnen, so schnell er eben kann,
Und stieß mit seinem Horne den letzten Schneidersmann.
Da fielen sieben Schneider pardauz auf ihre Nas
Und lagen beieinander maustot im grünen Gras.

Und sieben Schneiderseelen, die sah man aufwärts schwirr'n,
Sie waren anzuschauen wie sieben Fäden Zwirn.

74.
Wilhelm Busch, the nineteenth-century German cartoonist, invariably used a dynamic line. It was never a gesture only, but always gained its power through the shapes which it made.

LINE

Line, though hardly found in nature, is a primary element in much instructional visual material. Line cannot help clarity for long viewing distances, but it has a major role to play in describing shapes and details and making them recognisable - it literally delineates.

It is vital, for example, in historical illustrations, medical drawings, engineering cut-aways, graphs and charts.

People are more likely to agree in their interpretations of lines in terms of human behaviour than they are about colour. Douglas Sandle, a psychologist specializing in perception, has written that, 'big curved lines are in general experienced as lazy, dead, gentle, sad, whereas small curved lines are regarded as lively, playful, merry and so on'.

Designers and artists also know about the qualities of different types and strength of line and line patterns; yet, it is my belief that, although lines do have this rich expressive potential, they will remain merely decorative marks unless they contribute dynamically to some overall rhythm, relationship or shape.

MOVEMENT

Man is highly tuned to movement. Response to and judgment of movement is as essential to our survival on the roads as it used to be in the jungle.

Because it intrinsically attracts and interests, movement is highly motivational.

The factors of movement and change are vital characteristics not only of living things but of many interacting physical matters. Yet, the perception of continuous movement may not be essential to our understanding of change.

In an experiment if was found that the understanding of the workings of a Bren gun trigger mechanism was more successfully achieved by still drawings and text than by film, even though movement was an intrinsic factor.

It is often wrong to assume that movement and colour must be used in instructional materials simply because they are obvious characteristics of the real phenomena. A still or sequence of stills might not only be cheaper but better for learning purposes.

For further comments on movement see the sections on Film and Television in Part 2.

Sequence of Stills

Sequences of stills are used in filmstrips, posters, overhead projectuals, etc. Often, the essential aspect of movement is the aspect of change. In this sense a sequence of stills effectively shows 'movement', the minor changes not shown are implied. But a self-evident relationship between stills must be kept. The amount of change left out must be gauged according to the learner's age or to how much he knows already.

An advantage of using stills is that they are often easier to design to exact requirements than animation or live action film.

Following this point, it is often not particularly useful to take stills from a film for, e.g., a filmstrip. Stills are best designed as single if related units. If stills are designed as a sequence the pictures can interact with one another to give a dramatic and expressive effect.

In the sequence of 8 wall posters (designed for French language teaching to 9-year-old children) (Figs 75-82) there is a deliberate change of viewpoint and perspective in each poster to convey the changes in emotional tension.

75-76. Wallposters for language teaching.

71

77

78

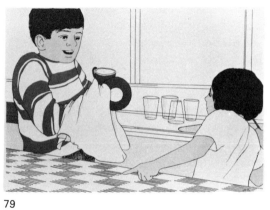

79

80

81

82

72

When the two children agree the lines are kept to the horizontal and vertical; when they disagree and dispute every horizontal and vertical line (except on the taps) is violently tilted and the pattern of the table cloth becomes a 'seismographic recording of anxiety'.

Movement within the Still Picture

This is a factor the layman needs a lot of convincing about, yet it is a vital cause of visual dynamism.

Movement in a Botticelli painting, in a Mondrian or in an 'op' art construction is a real thing.

De Sausmarez said in *Basic Design*, 'marks and lines should be appreciated as energies rather than as lifeless plottings'.

There is no reason why the most modest illustration, layout, credit or graph should not have this quality of force.

For some further comments on movement in the still picture see the sections on Shape and Line in this Part.

DRAMATIC IMPACT

Dramatic impact is more than just motivation. There should be as much involvement created by instructional materials as by a cowboy film, a music hall comedian, a Shakespeare play. The most mundane subjects like soap can be entertainment items, see the Unilever film, 'What is Soap', winner of many prizes.

The central advice given by audio-visual writers concerns clarity and logic, yet equally important is 'grip rating'.

REALISM TO SYMBOLISM

The preceding sections analysed design approach from the point of view of the potential of

83

84

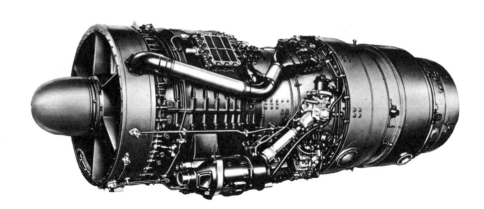

85

83-88.
Still photo, still photo close-up, airbrush artist drawing, cutaway drawing, diagram, pictograph. Each one of these types is used very specifically in Coplin's book on Jet Engines.

A proposed realism to symbolism dimension of representational types. The choice of representational convention is often quite arbitrary, partly because employer and even designer do not recognize the precise relationships of the various types and what they have to offer.

86

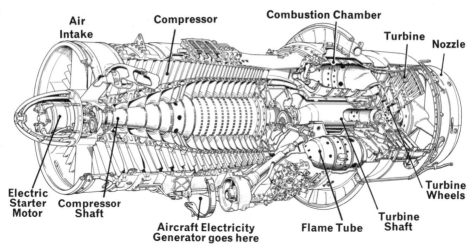

Air Intake

Compressor

Combustion Chamber

Turbine

Nozzle

Electric Starter Motor

Compressor Shaft

Aircraft Electricity Generator goes here

Flame Tube

Turbine Shaft

Turbine Wheels

87

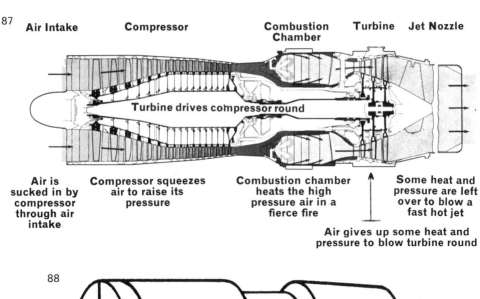

Air Intake   Compressor   Combustion Chamber   Turbine   Jet Nozzle

Turbine drives compressor round

Air is sucked in by compressor through air intake

Compressor squeezes air to raise its pressure

Combustion chamber heats the high pressure air in a fierce fire

Air gives up some heat and pressure to blow turbine round

Some heat and pressure are left over to blow a fast hot jet

88

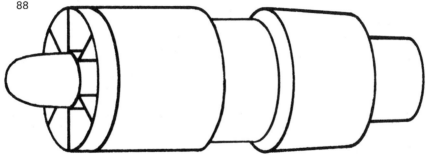

89

90

91

92

93

94

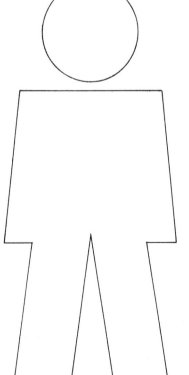

95

A MAN

96

89-96.
Photographic realism, selective realism, simplified realism, stylization, cartoon, stereotype, pictograph, word symbol. Which convention when? (see also Figs 4-8 and 13-19)

individual visual elements. Another way of considering which medium to use and how to design it may be based on the type and degree of realism which might be required.

No visual medium can be said to be totally realistic. Even stereoscopic colour movie film is a selective presentation decided on by the producer, the camera postion, etc.

The question, therefore, cannot be 'realism or not' but, 'how many and which visual characteristics of a situation it is necessary to show'. When presenting a new subject for the first time, it may be best to show every possible visual and sound feature associated with it, ie. as much realism as possible. Hence, a colour movie film or colour television would provide the answer. On the other hand, a more selective presentation may be preferable and a medium would be chosen in which only these important characteristics need be emphasized.

When a concept is well known it may be sufficient and most efficient to refer to it by a symbol or a pictograph.

Very often the degree of realism is wrongly pitched. Photographs are often used in language teaching when more realistic drawing would give more meaning to the new language. Sketchy, semi-realistic drawings are sometimes used of apparatus, eg. in chemistry, when stark, near symbol type diagrams would be less distracting. Colour movie films are used when movement is distracting and unnecessary, artist drawings used when high quality colour photographs would be more authentic.

The wrong degree of realism may cause distraction. An experiment to test the usefulness of still drawing in teaching was evolved. The drawing used showed the working of a Bren gun trigger mechanism. The need was to illustrate the relationships of the working mechanical parts; in this case, space, solidity and shape were the only necessary visual elements. The 'realistic' reference to the shinyness of metal, even if it had been well done, was a total and distracting irrelevancy.

It is essential to stress those visual elements which are going to convey the information and to play down or even leave out the rest.

Fig. 97 was used to teach Secondary School children aspects of a Cyprus peasant farm.

It was quite valid to use a drawing rather than a photograph, because what was required was a simple display of the shape, size and spatial relationship of the buildings. But the very qualities of selection and clarity, easier to achieve by drawing than by photograph, were missing. The buildings and the scene as a whole were obscured by irrelevant textures and details.

In any one subject there may be a need for every type of representation, from realism to symbolism. It is nonsense to say, for example, that colour slides or film are the best media for language teaching.

They are essential for cultural authenticity but, on the other hand, a highly specific and limited visual context may be required to give unambiguous meaning to new language. In this case an artist's picture may be able to present a more selective and controlled image by eliminating all irrelevancies.

At the far end of the realism - symbolism dimension there may be a need for the briefest of visual references which act as cues to remind the learner of what he has already learnt. In current language teaching methods a grammatical explanation is now often given only after

97.
A Cyprus peasant farm. Detail and texture have been used at the expense of shape and spatial clarity.

98. High speed photography. The splash made by a small object falling into water.

99. Would someone with something in his eye make head or tail of this?

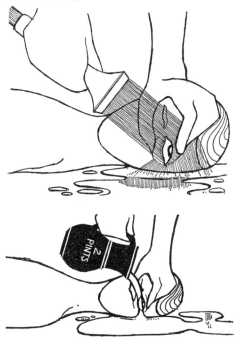

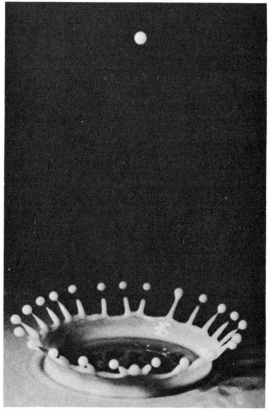

the language has been learnt and practised. A picture summarising what has been learnt at this stage of learning could, therefore, be a pictograph or stereotype.

Wrongly, but often, stereotyped drawing containing only decorative references or schematic references to light effects is used for the presentation of new language, when a visual type from further along the realism- symbolism dimension could have given a more real and lifelike context.

Photography and Drawing

The question of style frequently raises the choice between photography and drawing. Clearly, both media may be handled in many different ways, a near infinite variety of individual emphases can be made with the various visual elements.

Photographs may stress detail or form or be pure silhouettes. In educational terms, photography offers authentic reporting, bringing the real life example into the learner's experience, including the new insights given by microphotography, high speed photography, etc. (Fig.98) Photography tends to lend itself to an inventory of detail rather than to a selective and controlled presentation of formal elements.

There is no subject division of usefulness between photography and drawing. Drawing, both diagrammatic and illustrative, is as useful for the Science subjects as for the Arts. Medical drawing, machines, microscopic organisms are often represented by drawing rather than photography.

Both, photographer and designer can study an object and find 'perceptual pattern' but the designer, having more or less complete control over every mark, tone and colour on the visual, is often able to state more precisely and unambiguously what he has seen and felt to be relevant.

By simplifying shape, organising areas, giving emphasis and stating clearly three dimensional relationships, a drawing can convey an understanding of the subject, exact proportions, exact angles, concavity or convexity and distance between units.

Personal Style and Objective Requirements

More could be said about the qualities and uses of both photography and drawing. However, both are to do with marks on a surface and an objective analysis of the needs, in terms of visual elements, will help to make the decision of which to use and how to use it.

Unfortunately, objectivity is a problem. What balance can be made between the objective appraisal of the learning needs and the subjective make-up of the designer?

An objective decision on which visual aspects to use and which to emphasise need not cancel out a personal approach.

Unfortunately, very often, a personal approach does cancel out an objective approach. Many stylistic interferences could be illustrated here from all media, in book layout, film, drawing and photography. Fig. 99 is one example which, in my opinion, shows this strong interference by an artist's style. It is an illustration from a First Aid book intended for self instruction; very little is conveyed by the drawing except an extraordinary stylistic distortion.

GENERAL EDUCATIONAL RESPONSIBILITIES AND THE STEREOTYPE

The dictionary definition of stereotype is, 'something fixed or established in unchangeable form'.

Stereotypes are usually condemned but need they always be undesirable?

A stereotype, seen on the realism to symbolism dimension, lies next to the pictograph and symbol. Many stereotypes are highly naturalistic but the design and composition of the visual elements is in an 'established and unchangeable form'.

These 'ways of doing it' are accepted as ways of representing or signifying something and, in this sense, the stereotype is a symbol.

In education, marks and signs which are widely accepted as signifying something are useful. Why then condemn the stereotype?

When quick recognition of a well known subject is required the stereotype might be useful. But very often the stereotype is used in film, photograph, drawing and layout when a more specific and individual use of visual elements and a more specific and individual piece of subject matter would be better.

For many steps in the Teaching/Learning Sequence a particular or series of particular examples is required to help the learner to recognise the concept in its many forms in real life. To build up an adaptive classifying system, the learner must be supplied with varying examples.

The remarks above are not a condemnation of stereotypes but a caution about their limited applicability.

However, there are two aspects of much stereotyped work which are open to severe condemnation in educational terms, they concern form and subject depicted.

The subject depicted will not, in general terms, be the choice of the artist, but the examples may be.

A family group may be required but it is unlikely to be specified that Grandma should be white haired with pink cheeks and twinkling eyes; Grandpa a good natured old dodderer, father a square jawed Y-front he-man, mother motherly, daughter coy, sinewy, sexy, young son freckled and naughty - with all those hackneyed

Stereotyping of character, made even clearer by the horizontal cut.

100

ways of showing stance, turning of heads, gesturing of hands, flickering eyelashes associated with some advertising.

There is not much point in the educational designer fighting advertising art as such, but there is point in giving children (and adults, too) an alternative way of looking and of seeing the world. It is sobering to realise that people are conditoned to see the world increasingly by the criteria and ideas of the less original advertising art forms. We often 'see' in stereotypes and when the irregularities and 'uglinesses' of real life don't fit, we either pretend they are not there or condemn them.

One educational visual showed a teenage daughter thanking her father for a Christmas present. The artist had put her in profile so that one could see the fashion conscious flick of her hands behind her father's neck. Her back was arched, her head back, lips pouted in playful manner, last but not least, her leg cocked up with slipper half falling off.

In a small book like this such a lenthy description of a drawing is only justified by great importance.

The importance here is that pictures of this sort, repeatedly given in education, on television and in magazines, do condition people to behave and to see in certain ways; ways which do not help the individual to accept himself and others as individuals. Stereotyped responses help only in their deadening and not in solving the always changing problems everyone faces.

Stereotypes of formal presentation i.e. of shape, colour combinations, layout etc. affect people in a subtler way. Although by being familiar, they are easy to understand, they do not enrich the viewer's sense of form and his own ability to be visually creative.

Visual presentation must be clear and unambiguous, it must also be dynamic and imaginative.

To summarise: stereotypes as a form of symbol may sometimes be appropriate but, used too often, will restrict the learner's awareness of and response to his own environment.

SYMBOLS

People, particularly children, often have trouble in reading symbols. Before incorporating symbols into a design make sure that the intended receiver is familiar with them.

If this is not the case, the only alternative is that the learner is taught the meaning of the symbol before the visual is used. The designer cannot rely on this happening and in the case of self instructional materials it is obviously not possible, unless built into some introduction.

As previously mentioned (Part 1, The Learner) cross sections, process diagrams, graphs, charts and even some conventional diagrammatic symbols have proved difficult to interpret.

Research suggests that it is familiarity with the particular symbols rather than age or mental type which affects understanding.

When choosing symbols, use internationally accepted ones in an attempt to build up a useful international symbol language. (See Fig.101) When symbols must be devised, the following analysis of symbol types suggested by Rudolf Modley might help.

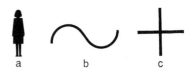

101. Modley's three categories of symbol.

Three symbolic representations of a soap molecule.

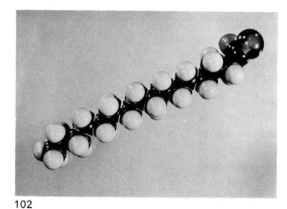

102

Deposited snow

Condition of snow surfaces

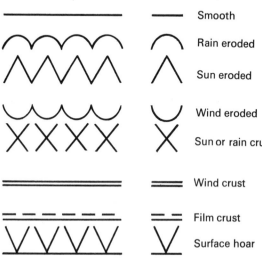

Smooth

Rain eroded

Sun eroded

Wind eroded

Sun or rain crust

Wind crust

Film crust

Surface hoar

103

$$CH_2 \quad CH_2 \quad CH_2 \quad CH_2 \quad CH_2 \quad CH_2 \quad CH_2 \quad C \overset{O}{\underset{O}{\big\|}} \quad Na$$

$$CH_3 \quad CH_2 \quad CH_2 \quad CH_2 \quad CH_2 \quad CH_2 \quad CH_2 \quad CH_2$$

104

International symbols striking an excellent balance between Modley's Image-related and Concept-related symbols.

Image related symbols or pictographs (a)

In limited circumstances and when the symbol must be self explanatory, a 'little picture' of the object is alright. However, it will lose validity if taken out of that context. In the case of Figure 101, this symbol is image related only in Western culture. It might well be interpreted differently in Africa or India or even in our own culture in the future.

Concept related graphic symbols (b)

This type of symbol is a good compromise. It contains recognisable characteristics of the subject, yet they are such basic characteristics as to be more cross culturally valid and less likely to date than those of the first category. Further, symbols of this type are easier to remember than those of the third category.

Arbitrary graphic symbols (c)

Owing to their total lack of visual reference they are more difficult to learn and to remember. However, once established, they are likely to be used for longer periods than any other types.

GRAPHS

Once more, this is a subject which is too wide for a small book. Yet once more, it might be useful to give some broad analysis and an indication of graph categories.

Graphs are widely used in instruction at all levels of ability and age, however, their usefulness is more limited than their use.

Area Graphs

This type of graph conveys the idea of broad differences of quantity.

Pie Charts

This type is useful for the idea of conveying fractions or percentages. However, small percentages cannot be shown easily and the eye cannot make an accurate comparison between similar sized slices. Words and figures printed on the slices often confuse and prevent the easy assimilation of shape differences.

Pictorial Statistics

This method, using a quantitative representation of small pictographs is useful when the aim is to attract as much as to inform. It is, again, not an accurate enough method to allow fine assessment and it may be difficult to make more than the broadest comparisons with other similarly represented statistics.

Bar Graphs

This type of graph has a wider application; several lots of data can be easily and accurately compared, both visually (comparing the top line of each bar) and by means of the figures on the two axes. Different colours and tones permit more information to be shown.

A misleading impression can still be given by changing the scales on the axes.

Line Graphs

This is the most useful type of graph, though it too, as all governments, newspapers, etc. know, can be designed to mislead.

It is a good type of graph because it is assessable at any point, the interaction of the two data quantitites are more accurately shown by this method than by the others. It also conveys a purely visual impression.

There are, of course, a variety of ways of designing line graphs according to whether visual impression or statistical information is the more important. The aim is often the former; in which case detailed provision for data assessment on the axes may be unnecessary and even distracting.

Three-dimensional Graphs

When the relationship between three factors is intrinsic to the idea to be communicated, then a three-dimensional graph becomes essential. A great number of separate two-dimensional graphs would be necessary to convey the same information and they might never succeed in conveying the same impression. And finally, it is 'impression' that graphs are about, based on an uncomplicated, visually symbolized relationship. Graphs are not for actual scientific measure, that must be left for the world of figures.

105. Area graph

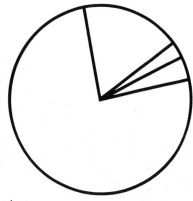

106. Pie chart

107. Pictorial statistics

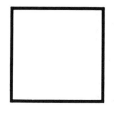

108. Bar graph

109. Line graph

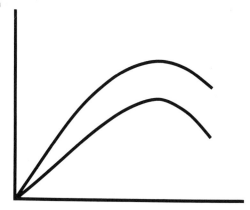

105-109. Six types of graph

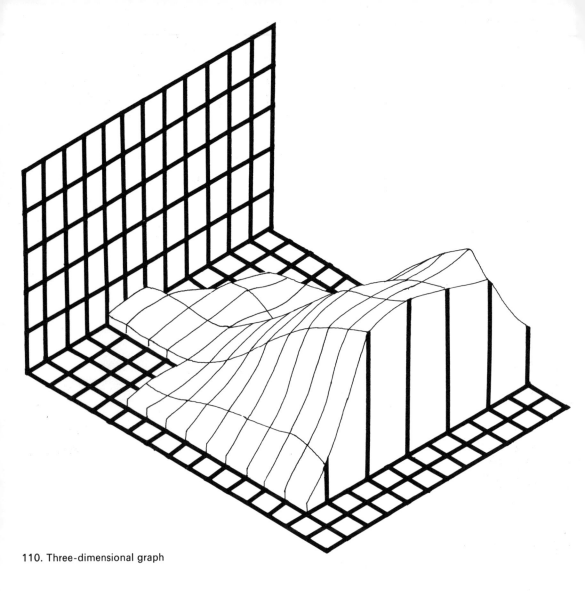

110. Three-dimensional graph

FLOW CHARTS AND BLOCK DIAGRAMS

Flow charts and block diagrams show the elements of a system and their relationship to one another. The elements are usually shown by boxes, and their relationship by lines between the boxes. In the case of flow charts these lines represent a flow of activity between the elements.

This rather conventional idea has received a new boost and a fresh application through the increasing development of an analytical approach in all subjects and through the development of totally new subjects, such as computer science, ergonomics and telecommucication. More could be made of block diagrams and flow charts in education, particularly if some basic sign types could be universally accepted. This was the point, very effectively made by Ken Garland, at a recent SIAD conference, and the following observations are largely based on his paper.

Garland compared the signsystems developed and used within various fields of similar study. It is quite clear from these comparisons that flow charts are often understandable only by a limited clientele within one subject area; and, even more surprising, 'in one instance, collegues on the same research project in the same department of a university were not able to explain one another's block diagrams with any confidence, because they were unsure about the exact meaning of some of the signs'.

A number of suggestions emerge from Garland's examination of flowcharts:

firstly, he proposes some general sign-types, (Fig. 111).

The disadvantage of the block flow chart, the most usual form, is that the verbal information determines the size of the block, hence the block size may be arbitrary. On the other hand, it 'gathers' the verbal information and is often necessary to avoid muddle.

The 'small node' convention is useful in those situations where

a. 'the direction of flow needs visual emphasis;

b. elements require varying lengths of descriptive matter which would otherwise cause disproportionate difference in the size of blocks; and

c. where typesetting is involved, since it is far simpler and more economical to set to a standard measure, and not to have to break up phrases in order to compress them within the shapes of the blocks.'

The main flow should be clearly and simply stated. Subsidiary movements, feedbacks, paths etc should not visually confuse the main flow. Some logic is also needed where there are 'yes' and 'no' alternatives, e.g. 'yes' lines could exit downwards parallel to the main flow, 'no' lines could exit towards the right.

The suggestions stress the need for a visual logic which is as important as a logical ordering of sequence.

WORD AND PICTURE

The designer should establish what commentary or text is to be used with the visual. In commercial film making sound and picture are tied together by the producer and director.

In the preparation of instructional materials there is often little 'tie in'; indeed, designer and subject writer may often be only vaguely aware of what the other is doing.

Proposals for general purpose sign-types to be used in block diagrams and flow charts

For use when lettering is to go within a box

For use when lettering is to go outside the node (preferred when suitable)

primary class of element

primary class of element

primary class of element outside main system

begin/first element in sequence/continued from...

begin/first element in sequence/continued from...

end/last element in sequence/continue to...

end/last element in system/continue to...

secondary class of element

secondary class of element

secondary class of element outside main system

decision: yes or no

decision: yes or no

main flow path

feedback path

boundary line

perimeter line of unit which includes two or more elements

111. Proposals for general purpose sign types to be used in block diagrams and flow charts.   *Ken Garland*

Generally, a divergence of text and visual will produce broken concentration and poor learning; for example, showing a picture of a Greek island when the commentary discusses climate statistics in the Mediterranean.

Commentary should be directly relevant to the image seen. It should direct attention and give emphasis; information added must be specific and limited.

LEGIBILITY (with letters as criteria)

Legibility will depend on the size of the letter related to the greatest viewing distance; on the degree of contrast; and on the readability of the typeface and the layout.

1. Letter size on projected and non-projected images

Kodak specify the following sizes and distances as a result of experiment. These assume optimum conditions, e.g. maximum contrast of letter and surface. (See Fig. 112)

Type size on artwork for projection:

How is the correct type size for use on the artwork to be estimated?

First, establish with the writer what the likely screen projection image size will be and the distance of the furthest pupil away.

If this cannot be established, the artist is advised to design for a specific size and distance and have this stated on the materials.

The image size and the viewing distance relationship usually recommended is 6W, i.e. the furthest pupil is not more than 6 screen widths away.

However, other relationships will work, providing the letters when projected, relate to the table below.

(Thus, for example, if the ratio is 10W, the lettering must be bigger on the screen than for 6W.)

Kodak have produced the following guide for artwork letter sizes related to screen size and viewing distance. (See Fig. 113)

2. Typefaces for projection

When working at the minimum legibility size, according to the table above, use a sans-serif medium weight face of normal proportions, e.g. Univers, Helvetica Medium, or in the USA, Tempo Bold and American Futura Bold.

The variation of letter thickness and the actual beards of serifed faces are not suitable for projection.

Extra bold faces tend to fill in; stencil letters, being rounded, become more ill-defined; condensed letters fill in, particularly if viewed at an angle. Typewritten faces are very indistinct.

Upper case or lower case?

Research into the effectiveness of various letter forms by road research teams favour lower case or a combination. All upper case, particularly for two words or more, is more difficult to recognize.

3. Line weight for projection

For graphs and tables Kodak recommend the following: minor rulings and grid lines in graphs should be about one half the thickness of the descenders of the type; major rulings in tables and date lines in graphs equal to the type line weight.

In tables use a double ruling for major divisions.

4. Layout for projection

Line spacing is an important factor for legibility Lines too close together will be hard to read.

112	Viewing Distance	Minimum height of lower case body (x height):
	128ft	4 in.
	64ft	2 in.
	32ft	1 in.
	16ft	1/2 in.
	8ft	1/4 in.

113	Distance of furthest spectator in screen widths:	Proportion of projected height of letter to height of screen:	Actual letter size on $6^3/_4$ in x 9 in artwork:	Actual letter size on 9 in. x 12 in. artwork:
	4W	1/75	.09	.12
	6W	1/50	.13	.18
	8W	1/35	.19	.26
	10W	1/30	.22	.30
	12W	1/25	.27	.36

114   **Letter height**

Smallest	140C		Pen No. 1
	Grid captions and scale numerals		
Medium	175C		Pen No. 2
	Part labels, symbol keys, etc.		
Large	240C		Pen No. 2
	Main title.		

Line Weights:

Light	Pen No. 00		(0.013")
	Grid lines, diagram details.		
Medium	Pen No. 1		(0.021")
	Borders, outlines of vessels and structures.		
Heavy	Pen No. 4		(0.043")
	Data and flow lines.		

A good starting point is to give a line spacing of $1^1/_2$ to 2 times the height of the upper case letters.

Between letters an en can be used between upper case letters and a thick space between lower case.

It is often best to centre text, particularly if each line can be a self contained sub-unit. A projected visual rarely contains a big body of text.

The main message is usually put above centre with the reading direction from top left to lower right.

5. Colour and tone for projection

The suggestions and tables given above are estimates for black and white images. Toned or coloured areas will have less contrast, letter forms and detail should, consequently, be bigger.

Although black on white gives the greatest legibility, according to tests, it is also straining for the eyes.

Further, marks and dirt show up very badly against a white area.

To reduce eye strain and signs of wear and tear, white lettering against a coloured surface, e.g. a dark blue, is very effective. For long distance viewing use a very rich colour to allow for loss.

6. Multiple-use artwork

(artwork for books and slides)

Slides made from books are usually unsatisfactory from the point of view of legibility, cf. serif typeface and a tight setting.

However, Kodak give the following advice when multiple-use artwork has to be designed: with a 6W viewing distance and 6 3/4 in. x 9 in. artwork using Leroy lettering apparatus. (See Fig. 114)

7. Typefaces for books

The empirically based decision of an experienced graphic designer is as likely to give an appropriate result as a decision based on the results of research and other recommendations. Research into the readability of typefaces is bedevilled by what people are previously used to, by personal preferences, by the variety of contexts, by changes of fashion.

Hence, some research is contradictory.

However, *A Psychological Study of Typography* by Cyril Burt and *The Visible World by* Herbert Spencer are worth reading, especially for their knowledgeable discussion of the character of the various faces.

For those designers new to or inexperienced in the field of typography the following recommendations could provide a reasonable guide for the selection of a face and size. For children under twelve: Old Style, and for the over twelves: Imprint, Times Roman and Plantin. For adults Burt suggests, as a result of his experience, 10 point Times New Roman and 11 point Imprint with two point leading, both in a measure between 20 and 30 ems. Two sans serifed faces, Gill Medium and Univers are found to be highly readable.

However, within reason, there are no radical differences in readability between the majority of well used typefaces for adults.

These suggestions are a starting point only; purpose and fashion are two major variables which might invalidate them.

With relation to these two variables:

when designing a book for sale abroad it might be useful to check what kind of faces are currently used. Faces and layout designed in one country may seem outdated, poor or even semi incomprehensible in another.

RESEARCH & THE DESIGNER'S WORK

Reading research findings helps to prevent the designer working on assumptions and, generally, getting into a rut. The results of research into some audio-visual topics are consistent and should be known by the designer.

However, much research, by its very nature, is only directly applicable to the unique circumstances in which it was carried out, i.e. with the particular students, particular teachers, particular way of doing things.

Therefore, do not be browbeaten, as a designer, by people wielding research results to prove that you are wrong in your intuitive judgements about your specific problem.

Further, it appears that much research has only been shakily scientific. 250 different studies, which had compared television instruction with direct teacher instruction, were analysed. The analysis concluded that 217 were 'uninterpretable', and 23 only 'partly interpretable' through defects in research design. Of the 10 remaining results no really significant differences in learning were shown between television instruction and direct instruction.

ORGANIZATION AND PRODUCTION

The freelance artist will often have no choice of media and no possibility of affecting materials. However, an increasing number of artists will be in a position to influence matters, for example in university visualization departments, government organizations, industrial educational divisions.

The artist will usually work in a team situation. Part of his contribution will be to channel and temper ideas according to practical realities - production time and costs.

The role that an artist plays is, of course, partly dependent on the goodwill and openness of his writer colleagues. However, an interested understanding of the subject matter as well as the criteria of Part 1 will allow the artist, including the freelance artist, to make a contribution far beyond what might normally be assumed to be possible.

BIBLIOGRAPHY

This bibliography is intended as a general guide to further reading.

R. Arnheim *Art and Visual Perception* Faber and Faber, 1954

M. J. Apter *The New Technology of Education* Macmillan, 1968

W. H. Baddeley *The Technique of Documentary Film Production* Focal Press

BBC Publications *What is Programmed Learning?*

A. Borger and A. E. M. Seaborne *The Psychology of Learning* Penguin Books, 1966

D. W. Broadbent *Perception and Communication* Pergamon, 1958

C. Burt, W. F. Cooper and J. L. Martin 'A Psychological Study of Typography' *The British Journal of Statistical Psychology*, Vol. VIII, May 1955

D. Bushnell *The Role of the Computer in Future Instructional Systems* DAVI

G. T. Buswell *How People Look at Pictures* Chicago University Press, 1935

Committee on Colorimetry of the Optical Society of America *The Science of Colour* Crowell, 1953

H. Coppen *Wall Sheets* NCAVAE, 1963

H. Coppen *A Survey of British Research in Audio-Visual Aids*, NCAVAE

P. Corder *The Visual Element in Language Teaching* Longmans

Council for Cultural Co-operation of the Council of Europe
   The Use of Short 8mm Films in European Schools
   Direct Teaching by Televison
   European Research in Audio-Visual Aids, Bibliography

E. Dale *Audio-Visual Methods in Teaching* Holt, Rinehart, Winston

Department of Education and Science *Audio-Visual Aids in Higher Scientific Education* HMSO

C. W. H. Erickson *Fundamentals of Teaching with Audio-Visual Technology* Collier-Macmillan

T. Gibson *Experiments in Television* NCAVAE

R. Goodman *Programmed Learning and Teaching Machines* English Universities Press

J. Halas and R. Manvell *The Technique of Film Animation* Focal Press

E. Herbert 'Technology for Education', in *International Science and Technology* August 1967

G. Kepes *Sign, Image, Symbol* George Braziller, New York, Studio Vista, London, 1966

G. Kepes *Language of Vison* Theobald, Chicago, 1951

S. Laner 'Some Factors Influencing the Effectiveness of an Instructional film, *British Journal of Psychology* Vol. 46, 1955

R. Laughton *TV Graphics* Studio Vista, London, Reinhold, New York, 1966

W. R. Lee and H. Coppen *Simple Audio-Visual Aids to Foreign Language Teaching* Oxford University Press, 1964

G. O. M. Leith *A Handbook of Programmed Learning* NCAVAE

P. Lewis *Educational Television Guidebook* McGraw-Hill

F. D. McClusky *The A/V Bibliography* W. C. Brown, Dubuque, Iowa, 1950

M. McLuhan *The Medium is the Massage* Penguin Books, 1967

G. Mialaret *The Psychology of the Use of Audio-Visual Aids in Primary Education* Harrap/UNESCO 1966

G. Mialaret *Psychology of the Use of Audio-Visual Aids* Harrap

E. Minor *Preparing Visual Intructional Materials* McGraw-Hill, New York, 1962

G. Moir *Teaching and Television: ETV Explained* Pergamon

P. Monier *The Complete Technique of Making Films* Focal Press

R. Ollerenshaw *Design for Projection: A Study of Legibility* Cambridge, 1962

National Committee for Audio-Visual Aids in Education *Closed Circuit Televison in Education in Great Britain*

Plenum Publishing Co. *Computer Graphics*, 1968

L. S. Powell *A Guide to the Overhead Projector* BACIE, 1966

L. S. Powell *A Guide to the 8mm Loop Film* BACIE

L. S. Powell *A Guide to the Use of Visual Aids* BACIE

Print (America's Graphic Design Magazine) *'The Designer and the Computer'* Nov./Dec. 1966

W. K. Richmond *The Teaching Revolution* Methuen, 1967

Arthur Lockwood *Diagrams* Studio Vista/Watson-Gaptill, 1969

P. Saettler *A History of Instructional Technology* McGraw-Hill, 1968

D. Sandle 'The Science of Art' *Science Journal* March 1967

B. F. Skinner *The Technology of Teaching* Appleton, Century, Croft, New York, 1968

J. Spear *Creating Visuals for Televison, NCAVE*

H. Spencer *The Visible World*

W. Schramm *People Look at Educational Televison* Oxford University Press

E. A. Taylor *Manual of Visual Presentation in Education and Training* Pergamon Press

UNESCO *Televison Teaching Today* HMSO

UNESCO *New Methods and Techniques in Education* HMSO

US Dept. of Health, Education and Welfare *Studies Related to the Design of Audio-Visual Teaching Materials* 1966

US Government Printing Office *Television in Education* HMSO

M. D. Vernon *The Psychology of Perception* Penguin Books, 1965

A. Vincent *The Overhead Projector* NCAVAE, 1965

C. Williams *Learning from Pictures* DAVI

H. Wiltshire and F. Bayliss *Teaching Through Television* Nottingham University

W. A. Wittich and C. F. Schuller *Audio-Visual Materials* Harper-Row

A. Wright 'The Role of the Artist in the Production of Visual Materials for Language Teaching' *International Journal of Educational Sciences*, Vol. 1, 1967

PERIODICALS

A/V Communication Review, bi-montly, DAVI
Audio-Visual Instruction, 10 issues per year, NEA (US)
Audio-Visual Language Association Journal, AVLA
Audio-Visual Media, International Council for the Advancement of Audio-Visual Media in Education, (ICEF), Pergamon Press, quarterly
Educational Television International, quarterly, Pergamon
New University and New Education London, bi-monthly
The Times Educational Supplement, London, weekly
Visual Education Magazine of the National Committee for Audio-Visual Aids in Education (NCAVAE), monthly

ABBREVIATIONS

NCAVAE   National Committee for Audio-Visual Aids in Education, 33 Queen Anne Street, London, W.1.

BACIE   British Association for Commercial and Industrial Education,
16 Park Crescent, Regent's Park, London, W.1.

DAVI   Department of Audiovisual Instruction, National Education Association of the United States, 1201 16th Street, N.W., Washington, D.C. 20036

HMSO   Her Majesty's Stationary Office.

ACKNOWLEDGMENTS

I am indebted to Mr Alan Haigh of the Leeds University Television Service and to Mr Edmund Franklin-White of the Hornsey College of Art for their assistance in the preparation of this book;

to Mrs Helen Coppen for her advice and encouragement,

to Mr Tony Becher and many others for their readiness to pass on their experience and advice.

I am particularly indebted to my wife for her help in the refining of my ideas and for the typing of the manuscript.

Also, acknowledgement and thanks to the following artists, designers, writers and publishers, who have kindly allowed their works to be reproduced:

E. J. Arnold and Son Limited (Fig. 55)

BBC North, Manchester; artist A. Wright (Fig. 51, 52, 90)

The British Film Institute (Fig. 27)

G. T. Buswell, *How People Look at Pictures*, The University of Chicago Press (Figs. 68,69)

J.F. Coplin, *Aircraft Jet Engines* Macdonald and Co. (Publishers) (Figs. 83-8)

Ealing Scientific Limited (Fig. 98)

Eastman Kodak Company, Rochester, N.Y. (Figs. 112-14)

Encyclopaedia Britannica International (Fig.73)

A. W. Gardner and P. J. Roylance *New Essential First Aid* Pan Books Ltd. (Fig. 99)

Ken Garland Esq. (Fig. 111)

Alan Haigh Esq. (Figs 4-8, 42-50, 61-3)

E. Herbert *Technology for Education* in 'International Science and Technology' (Fig. 57)

IBM (UK) Ltd (Fig. 58)

International Tutor Machines Limited (Fig. 56)

G. O. M. Leith *Learning from Abstract and Concrete Visual Illustrations* National Centre for Programmed Learning, University of Birmingham (Fig. 97)

D. G. Mackean *Introduction to Biology* John Murray (Fig. 71)

Macmillan and Co. (Figs 28-32, 33, 34)

The Nuffield Foundation/Schools Council Foreign Languages Teaching Materials Project, University of York

Figs 13, 14, 89 artist G. Reece,

Fig. 93   artist J. W. Taylor,

Fig. 92   artist R. Taverner,

Fig. 15   artist T. Ripley

Figs 1-3, 64, 65, 70, 75-82 artist A. Wright

N.V. Philips Gloeilampenfabrieken, Eindhoven (Fig. 21)

M. Sendak *Where the Wild Things Are* The Bodley Head (Fig. 72)

Shell International Petroleum Company Limited (Fig. 59)

Schools Council Project in English for Immigrant Children, University of Leeds artists M. Henley, A. Sier (Fig. 60)

Transart Limited (Figs 23-25)

Unilever Films (Figs 16-19, 36-41, 102-4) and also the material for the cover design

Westdeutscher Rundfunk TV, Cologne, Germany, artist A. Wright (Fig. 91)